The Raccoon Next Door

The RACCOON NEXT DOOR

Gary Bogue

Illustrations by Chuck Todd

Heyday Books • Berkeley, California

For Lois and Karl and the little striped skunk that cuts through my yard every night.—Gary Bogue

To Anita, Sienna, and Sheridan, whose love, support, and sacrifice made this wild project possible. And to my parents, Charles and Carol, who nurtured my passion for art.—Chuck Todd

Library of Congress Cataloging-in-Publication Data
Bogue, Gary L.
  The raccoon next door : creatures of the urban wilderness / by Gary Bogue ; illustrations by Chuck Todd.
      p. cm.
Includes bibliographical references.
  ISBN 1-890771-71-6 (pbk. : alk. paper)
  1. Urban animals—California. 2. Urban animals—California—Anecdotes. I. Title.
  QL164.B64 2003
  591.756'09794--dc22

                                        2003016122

Design: Rebecca LeGates
Printing and Binding: McNaughton & Gunn, Saline, MI

Orders, inquiries, and correspondence should be addressed to:
      Heyday Books
      P.O. Box 9145, Berkeley, CA 94709
      (510) 549-3564, Fax (510) 549-1889
      www.heydaybooks.com

Printed in the United States of America

10 9 8 7 6 5 4 3 2

Contents

Preface ....

The only purely scientific thing in this book is the scientific names for each of the animals I talk about. Most of the information, theories, facts, ideas, and sometimes out-and-out speculation behind what I'm going to cover in these pages has been derived from a wide range of pseudo- and non-scientific sources. These sources include my lifetime of work (I was collecting sow bugs and eating them before I could walk) as well as my personal research with native wildlife, which comprises a twelve-year stint as curator of the Lindsay Wildlife Museum in Walnut Creek, California; thirty-three years of reader surveys in my daily newspaper columns on pets, wildlife, and the environment for Contra Costa Newspapers (Knight Ridder Newspapers); and my daily devouring of scientific journals, newspapers, and Associated Press wire stories. Most important—and I can't stress enough how vital this part is—this book contains information derived from untold thousands of perceptive and knowledgeable reader comments, observations, and suggestions about their wild neighbors that have come to me over the years in the form of letters, e-mail messages, telephone calls, and personal discussions (and sometimes confrontations).

Most of the events and discussions listed here took place in the San Francisco Bay Area in Northern California, but they can just as likely occur in any suburban or urban community in the inhabited world. Only the colors of the feathers and the markings on the fur, or the shape of the head, or the sound of a particular animal's call are different. A raccoon is still a raccoon, a fox is still a fox, and woodpeckers of all species still peck holes in trees and powerpoles and buildings no matter where they live. Deer still browse through the middle of town at night and gobble up your roses, and the hawks, owls, and other predators that live where you live kill other creatures for food, just like the ones where I live.

When we humans decide to take over a natural area—a meadow, the pristine slopes of a mountain, the ridges leading up to that mountain, a wild tumbling creek, a pond—and we scrape, shape, alter, and mutilate it into our own artificial world, or into just another parking lot among thousands, the wild creatures that originally lived there have to leave. They are either driven away or killed if they can't relocate fast enough. And then, over the days and weeks and months and years, some of the castaway species gradually start to crawl, skitter, hop, wiggle, walk, and fly back into the remodeled suburban or urban environments. An unknown percentage of the displaced wildlife that returns will eventually adapt to living and sharing space with us two-legged beasties in this new half-human, half-wild animal world, but just how long that will take and how many different kinds of wild species will finally return to live with us are questions that are yet to be answered, if they ever can be.

I think a lot of the answer depends on the animals. Many creatures (black-tailed jackrabbits, gray squirrels, gray foxes, and legless lizards, to name a few) can only survive in specialized natural habitats completely unencumbered by our human trappings. Some (turkey vultures and mountain lions, for instance) are able to make short, regular forays into the urban wilderness before returning to their natural worlds. And others, like the opossum and the raccoon and the Eastern fox squirrel, thrive living in close proximity to us and our junkyards, garbage dumps, and huge bowls of pet food sitting just outside most of our back doors. Then there are those few, like wild turkeys and golden eagles, who can't quite seem to decide whether to live with us or not: in early 2003, reports of wild turkeys gobbling up suburban gardens and golden eagles perching on urban high-tension towers (and checking out the tasty house cats?) were increasing.

You will undoubtedly encounter more and different kinds of wild species if you live on the edge of town near an open space rather than amid the skyscrapers of a big city, where probably all you're going to see, other than the occasional raccoon, opossum, or rat, are a few sparrows, starlings, and *lots* of pigeons. Trying to figure out who your neighbors are when you live somewhere between these two extremes is what makes observing local wildlife the most interesting. It's also what this book is all about.

It offers some suggestions from me, and from thousands of readers of my daily newspaper columns, about how we can get along with these creatures—and they with us—without having to resort to throwing things at each other. For that reason, the animals in this book were picked on the probability that you might encounter any of them, at any time, in your front or backyards and, in some cases, as we'll explore later, even inside your house.

I'll bet that last part got your attention.

Introduction

Someone was poking around in your backyard last night.

Deer wander the streets after dark looking for tasty gardens. A barn owl swoops down and grabs a gopher on your front lawn when you aren't looking. And it's always such a surprise when you find a scorpion (hopefully one of the harmless ones) curled up under the birdbath.

This is just a glimpse of the whole other world of wild creatures living around us. As undeveloped lands give way to paved subdivisions and new homes, wild residents are being forced to coexist with their human neighbors or else relocate. But relocate to where? In many areas, there's no where there.

In this book, we're going to take a closer look at how some of the native wild creatures that live around us—your wild neighbors—are continually adapting to challenges brought about by urban and suburban development in the San Francisco Bay Area and beyond. What happens where I live is also happening wherever you live—just look around.

A Wild Housing Shortage

"There are too many houses being built around here," said the man who lives in one of them.

Of course we need more open space for the animals to live, but we also need places for the growing hordes of humans to live, too. The tricky part is getting the city and county governments to consider the needs of both animals and people in their land development plans. Look around and you'll see that doesn't always happen. Ha! What am I saying? It never happens.

Beautiful meadows where black-tailed deer and black-tailed jackrabbits once grazed peacefully become mammoth housing developments, and suddenly there is an "overpopulation" of deer "pruning" our backyard gardens. The natural creeks that once meandered around the valley and provided homes and breeding and foraging areas for fish, raccoons, gray foxes, and other wild creatures caused flooding problems for the non-native houses and thus were remodeled by our human flood control engineers into functional cement ditches. Most of the fish died and the animals that once lived in natural creekside habitats were turned out into the unnatural streets to spend the rest of their lives foraging in gutters and sleeping in the storm drains during the dry season.

Whole forests of ancient native oak trees are chainsawed and bulldozed from hillsides to be replaced by fancy plastic condo-miniums. All the animals that live in those oaks are evicted, and the territories of the other wild creatures for miles and miles around are disrupted by this brutal eviction process. It is particu-larly bad to remove a tree during springtime, because, besides the mammals and colonies of insects that live there year round, there are usually nests of baby birds perched in those protective branches. Almost everything lives in those big trees: squirrels, barn owls, great horned owls, screech owls, kestrels, songbirds of every feather and hue. Insects, so many that I don't have enough room to list them, are busy in miniature cities in the tree trunks and bark and branches.

When an open space is lost, we are evicting thousands of living creatures. Some will be lucky and find new homes nearby. Others won't survive. It's tough for a wild animal to find a home in the middle of a human city, and loss of habitat is a major contributor to the decline of many animal species. One day this problem is going to emerge from the ashes like a giant winged phoenix and take a great smelly poop on top of us humans. What goes around, comes around.

But you know what? There are still ways that wild animals and people can live together, if we more intelligent humans are willing to bend a bit and sacrifice some of our "ego systems." Wild ani-mals don't know any better, but people vote and lobby and pay taxes. We need to figure out ways to keep the present and ever growing labyrinth of roads and freeways from becoming huge walls that trap these animals (and us humans, too, you know) in what seem like giant holding pens. Wild creatures need to move about the natural environment and interact with each other if they are to survive. Larger animals, like deer, coyotes, and mountain lions, have to travel long distances to forage for food and breed with others of the same species so they can keep their gene pools from getting stale. Pockets of open space and parklands that still survive in our rapidly growing suburban and urban jungles need to be connected by open space corridors for this to happen. If you have open spaces where you live, please do what you can to preserve them. The wildlife are depending on you.

But getting along with our wild neighbors isn't always easy, especially if raccoon families are rolling up your lawn in a desperate (and we humans say destructive) search for tasty earthworms and playing loud tag games on your roof at night. Or hungry coyotes in your neighborhood are adding domestic cats to their diet. Or feral pigs, with the pent-up destructive force of a bulldozer, have destroyed your garden. Encounters with wildlife are simply no fun if you're on the receiving end of the vulture poop.

When most homeowners bump heads with one of their local wild neighbors, they're understandably in a hurry to fix the problem. Unfortunately, more than a few will opt for the "quick and dirty" solution: get a depredation permit from the state Department of Fish and Game and hire a hunter to blow away the pigs. Frighten the vultures away with a carbide cannon or take a shot at them when the game warden isn't looking. Smash the tarantula with a shovel. Live-trap a raccoon and dump the cage in a barrel of water to drown it. Yell into the telephone and demand that the Department of Agriculture send out a federal trapper to kill the coyote that ate your cat.

But these are all short-term answers that don't fix or resolve anything. Plenty of new wild pigs will be back again at the same time next year, and so will the young vultures, and hundreds of new tarantulas, hordes of new raccoons, and slinky packs of coyotes. In the end, killing one *resident* animal just makes room for even more *transient* animals to move in and take over its territory. It's not nice to fool with Mother Nature, you know. Why not look around for more long-term, humane solutions that actually work? Is it really so wrong to try to get along with your wild neighbors?

Of course not, so let's talk about it.

Songbirds

At just about any time of the day or night, you can hear or see wild songbirds somewhere around your house. By "songbirds" I mean those wild birds you usually see flitting about your trees and yard and visiting your bird feeders during the daylight hours. And, of course, they are usually singing their specialized bird songs. We can't forget the singing. I think that's sometimes the best part of a bird. How can you ever forget the first time you heard a mockingbird sing in a multitude of other bird voices? Wonderful!

Spring Bursts into Song

From out of the East Bay springs Mount Diablo like a giant green monument to spring. There is an invigorating richness in the air from the smell of young growing things and a crispness of vision after the March winds have blown away the dull winter sky. If you like green, this is your time of year. Everything is some shade of green, from the dark clusters of California poppies preparing to burst into bright golden bloom, to the softer green pillows of the hills, to the foamy green ocean of grasses roiling and boiling and tossing in rolling, windy waves along their slopes.

My favorite part of spring is the birds. They become so full of themselves and each other that you can practically walk up and tap them on their fluffy little shoulders before they'll notice you. The other evening when I was watering my garden with the hose, I almost stepped on a pair of mourning doves as they were cooing and wooing in the onions. I couldn't resist cooling them off with an icy spray of water. I know, I'm bad. So is the neighbor's gray cat that was playing Peeping Tom, checking out the action from behind the peach tree. I turned around slowly and cooled him off, too, with another burst. You occasionally need to assert yourself to let all your animal neighbors know who's really the boss of your yard.

In case you didn't notice, spring arrived this year, as it does every year, in a flourish of tiny trumpets. On the first morning of spring, millions of songbirds from throughout Northern

California and around the country lined the tops of your backyard fences like pastel birthday candles. They were waving colorful little flags and hoisting banners and miniature flagons of pyracantha berry juice to celebrate the vernal equinox, when the length of day and night, for just a heartbeat, are magically both the same. Too bad you missed it, it was quite a party. Man, that pyracantha berry juice is bad stuff.

Guess Who Was Dinner?

Birds have always had a curious effect on us grounded humans. Maybe we're envious because we can't fly. More than fifty million Americans feed backyard songbirds, says the National Bird-Feeding Society (my god, they even have their own society). That translates to more than one in five people in the United States, kids included. Do you know anyone who doesn't have a bird feeder in his or her backyard? On the slim chance you don't, I know a lady who has twenty feeders in her yard; I think that's kind of pushing the envelope.

You know your backyard bird feeding station has hit the big time when a bird-eating hawk stops by for a bite. When this happens, one second your yard is teeming with birds of every hue and feather, the squirrels are scampering through the treetops—and then, nothing. They've all disappeared. Songbirds, squirrels, and other prey species are fully aware of the life-threatening implications when a sharp-shinned hawk or a Cooper's hawk suddenly drops in for tea and a snack. If the hawk can catch a creature by surprise, you'll usually see it standing there on your picnic table with your favorite dove hanging from its talons, blood dripping from its beak. Otherwise, it's just looking around and wondering where everybody went.

The survival of the prey species depends on their ability to disappear instantly when a hawk zooms in to dine. The squirrel flattens itself against a tree and becomes one with the bark.

Songbirds dive into bushes, land on the ground and crouch in the grass, hide in the thickest leafy areas of trees, or zip around the corner of the house and into the comparative safety of a neighbor's yard. The trick is to not move, even for an instant. When the hawk scans the area with its sharp eyes, looking for prey, it is actually looking for movement. Blink an eye and you're hawk food.

When the predator finally leaves, it takes only minutes for your yard to once again be filled with songbirds and squirrels. They are soon pecking seed from your feeders and bouncing through the trees as if nothing had happened. As far as your backyard birds are concerned, nothing did happen. That's because survival is all in a day's work for the creatures that live in your urban or suburban jungle.

Where Do They Nest when the Trees Are Gone?

What does a bird look for in a nest these days? Locating and building a nest used to be pretty simple. All a bird needed was a tree or a bush, a nearby source of twigs and dried grass, and maybe a bit of dried lichen to gussy up the new place.

Oh, there would be minor variations, of course, depending on a bird's specific needs. If you were a twelve-pound golden eagle, for instance, you would have to make sure you picked a large tree or a solid ledge on the side of a cliff so it could support the platform of heavy branches needed to house your big, boisterous chicks.

If you were a tiny Anna's hummingbird, you'd need the end of a long, slender branch, so you could fasten your walnut-size nest made out of waterproof lichens and steel-strong spider silk where it could bob violently in the lightest breeze, making it virtually inaccessible to jays and other large predators that would like to eat your tiny darling youngsters.

Some birds that nest in areas where there are lots of mites and other parasites have learned to line the insides of their nests with the leaves of plant species that repel insects with their pungent odor. And nuthatches have been known to smear pine pitch and rub smelly insects around the entrance to their holes to discourage other insects from bothering them (see Reference List under *The Birder's Handbook*).

But in suburban and urban areas around the country, some of these natural nest-building materials are starting to change. It isn't always easy to find the right kind of tree or bush in the middle of town, so the nest makers have to do the best they can with manmade materials. Luckily, most of them do quite well, even if the outcome sometimes looks a little weird.

Mourning doves, for instance, have become particularly partial to raising their youngsters in the pots of hanging plants on backyard patios. Because doves have the dubious honor of being the lousiest nest builders since the dinosaurs (a mourning dove's idea of a nest is a piece of grass on a board, and when the wind blows the grass away, all that's left is the board), it seems the natural confines of those hanging pots come in real handy for a bird species that apparently never learned how to build a proper nest.

These strange living quarters also have the added benefit of protection from other animals. Birds that make such flimsy, uninsulated nests have to spend a lot of time sitting on them to keep their eggs and young warm, and this makes them vulnerable to predators. Nesting close to kitchen windows, however, appears to have given them a new kind of defense in the form of irate humans who come charging to the rescue at the first sign of danger to *their* doves.

Some hummingbirds have switched from building their nests on skinny branches to making them on wind chimes and dangling antenna wires, and house finches have moved from hollow trees into the vent holes in your attic. One oriole's nest found hanging like a cast-off sock in an oak tree near a Sacramento Delta marina was actually woven entirely out of clear plastic fishing leaders and monofilament lines. (There didn't appear to be any hooks.)

Birds pull off some amazing tricks to make their nests work. Most of the things they do are by pure instinct—like building a nest in a cactus to protect the babies from predators—but sometimes you have to wonder if our feathered friends aren't just a little bit smarter than we think.

One of my column readers found a robin's nest a few years ago in a grape vineyard in Escalon, in San Joaquin County, California. The exterior of the nest was made up of carefully woven strands of the orange plastic twine that field workers use to tie grape vines to trellises. The inside of the plastic nest was lined with the black nylon aviary netting that plant nurseries sell gardeners to keep birds out of their gardens and vineyards. In this context, the bright orange twine actually helps camouflage the outside of the nest from predators, and the black netting on the inside absorbs heat from the sun and keeps the baby robins warm while the parents are out foraging for food.

So where did that robin learn that black absorbs heat? Not everything always works out the way a bird figures it will when it decides to use something new to build its nest. I'm thinking about a crow's nest made entirely out of pieces of galvanized and copper wire that was found several years ago and taken to the Lindsay Wildlife Museum in Walnut Creek, California. Carefully crimped and bent by the powerful beak of the industrious crow that shaped it, the nest has not one single twig, piece of colored yarn, or bit of dried grass to its name. It is simply ten pounds of woven metal that has been beautifully sculpted into a modern art-deco version of a crow's nest. It is so perfect, and the thick pieces of wire are so weathered and realistically shaped, that I had to look closely to make sure it wasn't made out of sticks. But the thing's surprisingly heavy weight was an instant giveaway. No natural nest could ever be that heavy. No mere sticks could ever be that hard.

The nest was found perched on a beam above a false ceiling by workmen doing repairs at a shopping mall. Nearby was a broken window. This is the best sign I've seen to date that at least one species of native wildlife has finally devised a system to deal with humans' ever increasing destruction of its native habitat. Replace our trees with your houses and we'll build our nests in your attics, says the crow. Mow down the natural materials our ancestors used to make their nests and we'll rip out your electrical wiring and raid your scrap piles and build our nests out of indestructible pieces of metal.

As we busily go on wiping out native habitats and reshaping the wild lands to fit our own tame fantasies, more and more displaced wild critters are going to decide to move in with us. (If television reality shows stay in vogue, watch for *The Vulture Who Came to Dinner* in next fall's prime-time lineup.)

But some wild creatures have a way to go before that happens. Deep within the tangled, pointy wire folds of the metal crow's nest, if you look hard you can see the broken shells of the crow's eggs with a thick coating of dried yellow yolk. The broken pieces are poked full of holes from the sharp wires. The birds still need to get a few bugs worked out of using some of these new nesting materials.

Blackbirds ....

Every spring, Brewer's and red-winged blackbirds around the country act as if they're all trying out for the lead role in *The Birds II*. Blackbirds are very protective parents and will attack anything that gets too close to their nests. Cars, kids on the way home from school, neighborhood dogs, and innocent pedestrians get picked on—and pecked—every year during the spring nesting season. I once saw a huge bull galloping, twisting, and dodging around a field, trying to escape the aggressive antics of one of those feisty little birds. The bull could have squashed it with a flick of its ear, but for some reason seemed more concerned with defense than offense. Maybe he figured the blackbird knew karate.

You have nothing to fear from protective blackbird parents but fear itself. It's all an illusion, influenced in no small part by years of movies and television shows about heroes and heroines being attacked and pecked to death by killer birds. Not true! They may startle you when they initially swoop down out of nowhere, but in the end, the wimpy pecks from two ounces of black fluff won't damage anything but your self-esteem. Just hold a newspaper or schoolbook over your head; you can sneak away when the blackbirds stop to read it.

A friend recently spotted a couple of Brewer's blackbirds sitting on the front bumper of a neighbor's car. They were feeding off the dried bugs on the car's front grill.

They call it "bug jerky."

Brewer's blackbird
(*Euphagus cyanocephalus*)

I received a letter several years ago from a lady whose eighty-year-old mother lives by herself and tends her huge garden all day long. One day the woman looked out the window and saw her mom pruning her roses with a whole flock of Brewer's blackbirds standing around her feet in a large circle. They weren't the least bit frightened, but as soon as the woman opened the door to go out and join her mom, the birds "took off in a rush!" When she asked her mom what was going on, she just smiled and said, "You move too fast." She called the blackbirds "her boys."

Wild creatures are scared of things for a variety of reasons. Most are genetically programmed with a reflex behavior to automatically flee from natural predators. If you make a kite shaped like a soaring falcon and fly it over a flock of birds, they will take off in a rush or freeze on the ground, terrified by the shape of the shadow.

Some hawks will take advantage of this reflex and will dive down on ground-feeding blackbirds from out of the sun. If a hawk flies in just the right position relative to the sun, his shadow will pass over the grounded blackbirds slightly before the hawk himself. The result is that the blackbirds are frightened into flight...just as the hawk arrives overhead. The hungry hawk has then but to reach out to grab a footful of breakfast as it passes through the fleeing flock.

Learned behavior also plays an important part in developing an animal's fear response. If a dog chases a bird, for instance, the bird will learn to stay away from dogs, or maybe just *that* dog.

Sometimes the fear response can be quite specific—right down to individuals—but no one is sure what causes these lines to be drawn.

Animals also react to size. Understandably, little birds fly away from us big humans. But unlike the reflex fear-response blackbirds have to hawks, some bird species can learn to be unafraid of nonthreatening humans, as was the case of the woman's gentle mother and her brood. This may also be because humans are not the birds' natural enemies.

People who garden a lot have been chuckling at all this, I'm sure. There are many gardeners who have to shove birds out of the way with their shovels so they can plant something. Fear, and lack of fear, are very complicated emotions (reactions? reflexes?), and I've only just touched the tip of whatever it is that makes them work. If you want to learn more about what's going on, go find somebody's mom and spend the afternoon gardening with her and "her boys."

Red-winged blackbird (Agelaius phoeniceus)

Red-winged blackbirds are denizens of the open fields and wetland areas. If you live near such an open space, don't be surprised if you see out the window some morning a flock of these beautiful, flashy birds pecking around on your lawn.

One morning I opened my back door to call our Shetland sheepdog, Lady, to get her breakfast and saw the old dog was fast asleep in the middle of the yard...surrounded by a flock of about fifty red-winged blackbirds. Lady was so fast asleep that the foraging birds swarmed around and up and over the dog as if she were a big rock. She didn't seem to feel a thing, and the birds obviously didn't have a clue that the rock was actually a living creature that might leap up and run around frantically barking and chasing them out of *her* yard.

I didn't have the heart to spoil that beautiful effect, so I decided to call Lady for breakfast later, after the blackbirds had gone, and I went back in the house to have another cup of coffee.

Doves ....

Mourning dove (Zenaida macroura)

One of the best fathers I ever knew was a little gray mourning dove.

It's almost impossible to tell the sex of a mourning dove (unless you're a mourning dove yourself) because the males and females look so much alike. Once, when a pair nested in the pyracantha bush outside my home-office window, I got lucky; I saw the female laying eggs and noticed the male had a tiny white mark on his left wing.

For the three weeks they were building their nest, incubating the eggs, and starting to raise their young, I spent more time gawking out the window than I did at my computer keyboard.

They made a wonderful couple. The male brought his mate little sticks and pieces of grass and stood there patiently holding them in his beak while she fussed around to make them fit just right. She once spent ten minutes fooling with one crooked twig, and when she finally paused with a frustrated look on her beak, the male quickly handed her a new stick and dropped the crooked twig on the ground when she wasn't looking.

For the two weeks they incubated their two eggs, he was the perfect model of a father-to-be. They took turns sitting on the nest in approximately twelve-hour shifts, and I'm sure he was always early for his shift. When she was on the eggs, he would show up regularly and regurgitate seeds from his crop into her open beak, just like he would soon be doing for the hungry babies when they hatched. Sometimes he'd just sit on the side of the nest and spend the afternoon snuggling with his lady.

The female dove always took the early dawn shift. When the two chicks hatched, I'd stand there with my morning coffee and watch her fluff herself around them like a giant feather pillow to keep them warm. And when the male took over for the night, he did exactly the same thing and that was kind of neat.

One morning I found the male dove caring for the chicks. His mate was gone and we never saw her again. I have no idea what happened to that dear lady. A hungry hawk? A despicable cat? The unyielding fender of a speeding car? We'll never know.

It's at least a good thing this didn't happen while they were incubating the eggs. The male would never have been able to keep the eggs warm all by himself and still forage for food. Even now, I'm not sure how he managed to peck enough seeds to keep himself alive, let alone provide for the needs of two ravenous growing babies. But he did. And he did it without once looking frazzled, or losing his temper, or getting a single feather mussed out of place, or coming home drunk one night and storming around the nest and telling the kids what brats they were.

And then one morning they were all gone.

I'd been expecting it. The two chicks had been testing their wings for the last few days while their dad sat on a nearby branch and proudly watched. I smiled as I finished my coffee. I knew they would be fine because their father had cared enough to devote his life to making it so. The female, bless her little lost heart, would have been proud.

Listen to the Wind

Have you ever wondered what causes the whistling sound made by mourning doves when they fly? The sound is caused by the wind whistling through the feathers as the doves flap their wings. All bird wings make sounds to some degree, some soft, some loud (you should hear a woodcock!); it all depends on the particular shape and configuration of the wing feathers.

The high-pitched whistling of mourning dove wings varies in frequency with the wing beats, such that I can tell the doves are landing below my bird feeder without even turning around.

Finches ....

American goldfinch (*Carduelis tristis*)

This yellow gem of a bird with the crisp black cap is one of the brightest jewels to be seen at your bird feeder (that's the male; females are olive-yellow and don't wear caps). Fill your feeders with thistle seeds if you want these flashy birds to stick around for a while so you can enjoy them.

(Don't forget you'll also need a special feeder with teeny holes in the side to hold the tiny thistle seeds.)

House finch *(Carpodacus mexicanus)*

The house finch is probably our most common feathered backyard neighbor. The female finches wear light- and dark-brown streaks and are always hanging out with those colorful males, whose heads and breasts are painted in various shades of red. This species prefers to nest in your attic vent holes, birdhouses (so why don't you go make one with the kids?), and in other nooks and crannies around the house.

Speaking of Finches

Each December, a lone house finch takes up residence on a drainpipe not too far from a friend's front door. The drainpipe curves under the eaves next to a wall and is protected on one side by a lower eave. My friend says it's a pretty snug little spot that stays dry during the wettest winter storms. The finch has been returning to spend its nights roosting on her drainpipe during the winter season for the past six years. "It just makes my heart glad," my friend says.

Curious, how one little bird can sometimes bring back a whole host of special memories when you see it. A huge Northern flicker returns to my backyard every fall. I know he's back when I'm awakened early one morning by his awesome loud screech as he tells the world that he's home for his annual fall visit. Like my friend and her house finch, it just wouldn't be the same without the comforting knowledge that all is right with the world because "our flicker" has returned for the winter. It's the same when the flocks of American goldfinches arrive to enliven my thistle seed feeders with their flashy greenish-yellow suits.

We're always talking about our companion animals not liking changes in the ritual of their daily lives (breakfast at 7 a.m., nap at 8 a.m., noon sun bath, nap at 1 p.m., nap at 2 p.m., etc.). I think we humans are just as bad, if not worse. When I stagger out of bed in the morning and look out the window to see our flicker sitting on the fence under the apple tree and the goldfinches perching on the bare limbs of the peach trees like little Christmas tree lights, it makes me feel like everything is okay. The year can now move ahead into its fall and winter modes.

That's just one of the roles the house finches and flickers and goldfinches and all our other wild neighbors can play for us. It just makes our hearts glad to know they are around.

Hummingbirds ....

Hummingbirds amaze me.

Once I found a deserted hummingbird nest and sat down with it under a bright light with tweezers and a magnifying glass. The walnut-size nest turned out to be an architectural marvel. The outside of the nest was covered with a waterproof layer of lichen and spiderweb. The inside was filled almost to the top with lint, non-sticky web, and other wonderful softness. The upper rim of the nest curved sharply inward all the way around the topside. This overhang had a springy quality, probably because of the flexible, tensile strength of the web. This elastic lip was what allowed the nest to fit protectively around the mama hummer during a storm, like a sleeping bag with a drawstring around the top. Mama keeps herself (and later the babies) from being tossed out of the bobbing nest during the windstorms by hunkering her shoulders down under that lip and hanging onto the lint and spiderweb in the bottom of the nest with her feet.

Before leaving to feed (about every fifteen minutes because of their super-high metabolisms), hummers tuck their eggs into the insulated lint nest bottom where they stay warm from the mother bird's lingering body heat until she gets back. Her own multiple layers of overlapping feathers provide her with a fancy green raincoat that keeps her dry when she feeds.

So there you have it. A waterproof, magically camouflaged, perfectly insulated nest made of all-natural materials. And it was designed and constructed by a thumb-size bird that never took a single drafting class in college.

The San Francisco Bay Area is right in the middle of an aerial highway known as the Pacific Flyway. During the fall, winter, and spring months, migrating birds pass back and forth above the area on their way north or south. It is not uncommon for individual birds or whole flocks to stop off for a bite to eat, to refuel their feathered tanks before continuing on their merry way. This activity often contributes to some interesting short-term visitors to your backyard hummingbird feeders.

The most common hummer in the Bay Area is the Anna's hummingbird (mostly green). Not so common, but still around, is the Allen's hummingbird (green with some red), followed by the even-less-common Rufous hummingbird (mostly reddish). But hummingbirds are adventuresome souls, and even black-chinned hummingbirds are known to occasionally drop by for a quick snack.

Allen's hummingbird (*Selasphorus sasin*)

Being up close to such a vibrant life force is always exciting. And these tiny birds have a huge curiosity about everything and very little fear of anything. My favorite Allen's hummingbird story comes from a lady (who prefers to remain nameless) who was taking a topless sunbath on her back patio one hot June afternoon. As she was lying there broiling under the sun, an extra-thick coating of bright red lipstick on her lips to keep them from getting chapped, she felt a tiny shivery tickle on her lips. Carefully opening one eye, she found herself staring at a male Allen's hummingbird that was hanging in the air mere inches from her face—tasting all over her bright red lips with his tongue.

She said that when his eyes met hers, the little rascal gave her a very big wink. Honest.

Anna's hummingbird (*Calypte anna*)

Anna's hummingbirds are the biggest group of nectar feeders in your backyard (let's not forget the fifty-one other species of songbirds around the country that are known to sneak in and grab a quick sip from your feeder now and then when they think no one is looking). A male Anna's hummingbird usually protects *his* feeder from other hummingbirds, and sometimes other songbirds, and even from the human who is trying to refill the feeder.

Anna's hummingbirds are tough little characters and among the first birds to breed every spring, often laying eggs as early as December. The eggs hatch in fourteen to nineteen days, and three weeks later the youngsters are off and on their own.

Their nests are usually constructed on a low, skinny branch that whips about in the wind or else somewhere on the patio where we humans do our thing. All this action and activity frightens away the scrub jays and other birds (and cats!) that try to raid their nests. An Anna's hummingbird also picks a spot for her nest because she likes it. There's usually plenty of food in nearby nectar feeders, plus insects and early-blooming flowers here and there.

If you happen to be watching a family of hummingbirds, don't do anything to try to help the mother raise the babies. You'll just get in the way. Back off and enjoy those tiny feathered "flowers" as they bloom with new life.

A Spring Blossom

The tiny Anna's hummingbird started building her nest a little over a week ago, give or take a beakful of spiderwebs. I was standing on my back deck enjoying the misty rain when I spotted her bouncing up and down around the trunk of the apple tree like a tiny green Tinkerbell. She had her beak full of white fuzz that caught the light of the early morning sun and made it look like she was wearing a shimmering halo.

Everything those delightful little characters do is heavenly, I chuckled to myself.

After filling her beak with web, Tinkerbell would zip across the back lawn and into our little grove of three redwood trees in the corner of the yard. I waited until she was out of sight, taking a snack break at the feeder, and ran over to the redwoods, carefully parting the branches at the spot where she kept disappearing to. After a minute, my eyes adapted to the shade and I spotted the nest—a lichen-encrusted "walnut" at the end of a branch, open at the top with wisps of web sticking up here and there. It was a work in progress—a functional sculpture—a piece of natural live-in art. Eat your heart out, Frank Lloyd Wright. And it was almost complete.

I was startled out of my reverie at the sudden "Tich! Tich! Tich!" in my right ear. I slid my eyes sideways and found myself staring into Tinkerbell's pinpoint eyeballs as she hovered inches away. She was so close I could hear the loud hum of her wings and feel their wind against my cheek. Tiny beads of water from the misty rain were scattered all over her back like precious jewels.

"Sorry," I said, slowly moving away from the nest. She escorted me back across the lawn and up onto the deck, then zoomed around to continue her search for spiderwebs in the wild desert canyons of the apple tree trunk.

For the rest of the week, I did most of my watching after I got home from work. In between doing my chores, I'd spend a few minutes at the kitchen table by the window, using binoculars to watch the lovely Tinkerbell in action. Occasionally, when the hummer dashed off to feed herself, I'd slip out with my big magnifying glass and examine the nest for any new stitches she'd added with her slender knitting-needle beak.

The nest had become a truly beautiful thing to behold. It was a fragile teacup, a little over an inch in diameter. The top edge had been curled slightly inward, as if pulled by a drawstring to fit over the backs of baby hummers to keep them from falling out of the nest. The outside of the treetop cradle was a collage of lichens, leaf bits, and teeny twigs, making it almost impossible to see. A little hummingbird needs to take every advantage to survive in the big world.

Last weekend, Tinkerbell laid two eggs. I spotted her sitting in the nest on Saturday, her rapier beak jutting up at a cocky angle as if to say, "I did it!" What a sweetie!

On Sunday, I stared at the empty nest in stunned disbelief. Tinkerbell was gone. All day I watched for her in vain. No little warm green bird. No cocky, slender beak. Just two cold eggs containing what might have been.

It's the next morning now, and something has eaten the eggs. I have no idea what happened to the hummingbird but I know only death could keep her away. Spring has finally come to my yard but its very first blossom is gone and the rest of the garden has not yet begun to bloom.

Epilogue: I found the body of the little female Anna's hummingbird lying under the apple tree last night. I think the wind made a giant fist during a recent spring storm and smashed her from her favorite limb. She seemed so peaceful lying there in the dirt next to the bird bath. I hope it didn't hurt. I found a nice spot by the grapevines and poked a hole in the soft wet earth with my thumb and buried her under a leaf that had also fallen from the apple tree. I'll miss that little lady. The yard won't be quite the same.

How to Be a Good Hummingbird Neighbor

Hummingbirds *hate* the taste of chlorine. The first time I cleaned my hummingbird feeder with a mild solution of bleach and water, I was in a hurry and forgot to rinse it out afterward. The hummer landed on the feeder, started to take a long sip, and immediately yanked its beak out of the hole and spit the nectar out. Phooey! Since then, I've always been careful to rinse out the chlorine taste. I've checked over the years, from time to time, to see if other individual hummingbirds reacted with the same response to that flavor. They do.

Clean your hummingbird feeder well about once a week with soap and water, dry it in the sun, and then refill it with a solution of nectar (four parts water to one part granulated sugar, which approximates the sugar content of many flower nectars). There's no need to add red food coloring to attract them because it just stains their tail feathers when they defecate and gives them red taillights when they don't need them. Today's hummingbirds know what store-bought feeders look like.

Jays ....

Mother Nature is a lady of many contradictions. Although Steller's jays and scrub jays frequently prey on young and injured birds, these hyper-aggressive creatures also have another role in Mother Nature's grand scheme of things: they are the treetop lookouts of the forest (which also includes your backyard). This job appears to take precedence over all their other tasks, as the jays are very serious about alerting birds and other animals when there's trouble a-foot or a-wing.

They scream at two-legged, two-winged, and four-footed predators whenever they spot them in the area, the intensity of their squawking signifying the seriousness of the problem. Other birds of every species, voice, and hue then immediately rally to the trouble spot and you soon have a screeching aerial mob diving and harassing the hawk or house cat that was foolish enough to think it might sneak up to catch a bird for dinner without being seen by the ever alert busybody jays.

A lot of careless birds also owe their lives to the jays for attracting a human to frighten off the cat. But let's hope those birds didn't stop to thank the jays. That could spoil everything. Jays have to eat, too, you know.

Western scrub jay
(Aphelocoma californica)

Nothing looks more bedraggled than a soggy scrub jay.

Last summer I taught my son Karl how to get a scrub jay to fly to his hand for a peanut. Soon, he had two jays—the Blue Brothers, Mr. Blue and Azule—taking peanuts from his fingers and hiding them all over the yard. (Our cats wouldn't speak to Karl for a month.)

The other morning rain was pouring down as if out of a large pitcher. It was just getting light and I was making a pot of coffee when I heard a funny noise. I turned to see Mr. Blue standing on the deck in front of the sliding glass door. I have never seen a bird so wet. The wind tossed raindrops at the glass door so hard that they sounded like gravel. I could see the drops hitting the jay, knocking his usually sleek blue feathers all helter-skelter.

I got some peanuts from the bowl, knelt in front of the door, and slid it open several inches. Mr. Blue squished through the opening and stood looking up at me, his beak almost touching my nose. He gave a small squawk.

"Keep your voice down," I whispered. "You'll wake the cats."

He took a peanut and sloshed back out the door, returning two minutes later with his beak and breast feathers all covered with mud. That idiot had gone out and buried the peanut in the rain!

Ten peanuts in all disappeared in the same manner. When he saw they were gone, so was Mr. Blue. All that was left was a big puddle of muddy water on the linoleum. I turned to get some coffee and found two cats glaring at me through slits of eyes. Oops.

How to Hate a Jay

Keeping the scrub jays well fed might slow them down a bit, but it probably won't stop them from preying on baby birds when they get a chance. Anthropomorphically speaking, scrub jays are a

Jekyll-and-Hyde mix, kind of a cross between a songbird and a hawk. They are both scavengers—eating everything from seeds to fruits to garbage—and hunters—preying on insects, baby birds, and lizards, and I've even seen them catch mice. We humans don't like it one bit, but we can't stop them from being what they are. Watch the Discovery Channel some night and you'll probably feel the same about hyenas and wild dogs.

Yes, jays can be frustrating, especially when they raid a nest of baby hummers right outside your daughter's bedroom window and she wakes you up with her screams early one morning as my own daughter did many years ago.

Yet even though our feelings won't stop jays from playing their roles in the local environment, under Mother Nature's complex directions, that doesn't deter some people from getting emotional. I knew one man who got so angry at his local scrub jays that he spent every spring trying to fool them. He made carefully researched bird nests, tied them in trees in his backyard in just the proper spots, and then carved little eggs out of Styrofoam, painting them the correct colors for the eggs of the bird species he was imitating and putting them in his artificial nests. He used to sit on his back deck with a can of beer and cackle with laughter as the jays tried to break the eggs.

Steller's jay (Cyanocitta stelleri)

A man in the Seattle, Washington, area wrote me to describe some Steller's jays that always reacted in a curious way when the man tossed peanuts on his lawn to feed them. Each jay would fly down and pick up a peanut, then drop it and go pick up another peanut, then maybe go back to the first peanut, or another peanut, and pick it up, as if trying to decide which of the peanuts it liked the best. The jays would sometimes go back and forth between three and four peanuts before finally finding one that was acceptable (sometimes the first one!) and flying off to hide it. The man wanted to know what criteria the jays were using to decide which peanut was the best.

An amazing number of my readers responded to this question with similar stories of their own. All believed their jays (a mix of scrub and Steller's jays) picked up peanuts to check their weights, figuring the heavier peanuts contained more nutmeat for them to eat.

This theory seemed to be verified by one clever gentleman who weighed a selection of peanuts on a balance scale and placed them in a row on a table in his patio, arranged from heaviest to lightest. On four different tests, jays checked through the different peanuts and picked the heaviest one to eat 63 percent of the time.

Mockingbirds ....

Northern mockingbird (Mimus polyglottos)

Mockers either sing more beautifully than a nightingale or make a racket that keeps you up all night, depending on who you ask. All male mockingbirds sing during the day, but only the bachelors sing all day *and* all night, so you can guess what it takes to shut these guys up. Females pick the males who can sing the most songs, even if

one of those songs sounds like the ringing of a cell phone.

American Songbird Idol

It's time for the Fifth Annual Gary's Mocker Remedy Contest!

Over the last century or so that I've been writing my daily newspaper column, I've gradually discovered there is a delightfully randy mix of mockingbird lovers, haters, and just-barely-tolerators out there in never-never land. For some reason, a lot of people seem to have trouble dealing with a little birdie that sits on their roof and sings its heart out "all (expletive deleted) night long" for days at a time. Can you believe that some people actually have trouble sleeping when a mockingbird is singing? It puts me to sleep like a lullaby.

Five years ago, after a librarian friend alerted me to the fact that every single copy of *To Kill a Mockingbird* in every East Bay library had been checked out, I decided to hold my first Mocker Remedy Contest to try to defuse the situation. The winning remedy in that first contest was rather elegant: "Just smile, relax, and enjoy it when a mocker keeps you up singing at night. Soon you will be sound asleep and you'll awaken in the morning all refreshed, instead of exhausted from a night of trying to kill a mockingbird."

We've encountered some pretty unique and hilarious ways to get along with mockingbirds since then. All in the spirit of good, clean fun—except, possibly, for the gentleman who flung aside the covers one dark night, grabbed his chainsaw while dressed only in a T-shirt (that's right, just a T-shirt), and cut down the sixty-foot Monterey pine in his front yard that had a singing mockingbird perched in the very tippy-tippy top. It's not often an entire suburban neighborhood gets awakened at 2 a.m. to the sound of "TIMBER you (expletive deleted) feather dust mop!"

Unfortunately, not everyone is for the birds, and mockingbirds, as you now know, make some people go absolutely crazy. A couple of years ago, another reader wrote to me about her father's war with a mockingbird that was singing all night and keeping him awake. He finally couldn't stand it any longer and got up in the middle of the night, grabbed a chainsaw, and cut down the tree it sat in. But the next night, the mockingbird started singing again, this time from the top of the guy's old TV antenna. So the man got up and cut down the TV antenna with a hacksaw. The reader said she didn't hear a thing after that. I've often wondered if the house is still standing.

Another man became so enraged at a mockingbird's midnight arias that he stayed up recording its songs and then replayed them out the window at maximum volume through a pair of huge Dolby speakers. The mockingbird was never seen or heard from again. The only thing left was just a few gray and white feathers seen blowing across the man's driveway.

Still, by far the best letter out of the 531 entries to my first four Mocker Remedy Contests is this wonderful epistle from Robert J. Richey of Concord, California:

Dear Gary:
After losing several nights of sleep due to the nocturnal twittering and chirping of the infamous East Bay mockingbirds, I felt it

might help to offer advice to those who are new to the area.

The following remedies have proven unsuccessful:

Adding melatonin to the birdbath...fluffing the nest and leaving a chocolate truffle by its pillow at bedtime every night...cannon-blast sound effects from the *War of 1812 Overture*...playing loud music next to their nesting area during the day...strategically placed pictures of a *Tyrannosaurus rex*...videotapes of *Cosmos with Carl Sagan*.

Under current study, but still unproven:

Beak muzzles that allow only humming... new designs for mockingbird lingerie... plastic blow-up life-size female mockingbird dolls...laser-guided bowling balls.

I love those birds.

Orioles ....

Bullock's oriole (*Icterus bullockii*)

Orioles are the next most frequent visitors at your hummingbird feeder, after the hummingbirds, of course. When you hear an oriole's loud stutter-call, run to the window immediately and watch the hummer feeder for a colorful circus act as a big oriole tries to get a foothold on the hummingbird-size feeder to drink some nectar without spilling it all over his breast feathers. Someone eventually got around to putting some special oriole feeders on the market so they'd stop spilling the sticky nectar all over your patio, but since they're nothing more than hummer feeders with little perches for the clumsy orioles, I just use oriole feeders in my yard. If you peek out your window at the right moment, you'll see that the hummingbirds also like to use the perches to get a little rest now and then. (I know, there goes their macho image, right?)

Clever Birds

A woman in San Pablo, California, dropped me a note describing how orioles figured out how to use her disk-type feeder with drinking holes on top and places to perch around the sides. She described how first the finches and then the orioles dealt with not being able to push their bills far enough into the holes when the nectar level dropped. The heavy orioles just bounced on the feeder. They'd hop into the air, turn, and come down hard on one of the perches. This would make the feeder swing back and forth, causing the fluid to slosh up through the feeding holes where the orioles could grab a quick drink. It was kind of labor intensive, but they were eventually able to drink their fill—in time.

The smaller and lighter finches learned to sit on one side of the feeder and drink out of the same hole together when their combined weight tipped the feeder and nectar in their direction.

To the orioles, our feeders are just a pretty ingenious snack food; they get most of their meals by sipping nectar from flowers (and eating some of the blossoms) and raiding fruit trees in neighborhood yards. My own resident orioles went berserk when our Santa Rosa plum tree started to bear large, ripe, juicy plums. They'd hang upside-down from the branches and slurp the innards out of the plums until their orange breasts were stained a deep purple. Want to make an oriole happy? Leave a few ripe orange slices sitting on your back deck railing. They love them!

Robins ....

American robin (*Turdus migratorius*)

Everybody knows what a robin looks like. We know it must be springtime when there's suddenly a robin sitting in the middle of the back lawn after a long winter. And we know this must be the early bird that always gets the worm because that's what we always see them pulling up out of the grass. Avian biologists wonder if robins see worms or hear them. When they cock their heads, it's pretty hard to tell if they're concentrating with one ear to try to hear a worm crawling or trying to focus on a worm with one beady black eye. When not confusing the biologists with their worm-catching, robins also eat fruit and insects and an occasional seed or three.

A reader once wrote me a long letter about "the most bizarre robin phenomenon I've ever seen!" At twilight on a cool February evening, she looked out her back window to see the trees in her yard swaying vigorously back and forth and then saw what she thought were bats swooping and flying from tree to tree.

"I stepped out on the deck to see better, and to my astonishment there was a flock of hundreds of robins—I'm not exaggerating, maybe even thousands!—swooping in to roost for the night. They were in the neighbor's trees as well. It gave me the Alfred Hitchcock chills!" The next morning, she said, the robins noisily took off into the dawn, "in a loud chirping frenzy."

It may seem weird to have huge swarms of robins sleepily chirping the night away in your backyard apple tree, but remember, a flock of migrating birds has to sleep somewhere. And as the natural fields and grasslands, rolling hills, marshes, and woodlands where the birds would usually stop are being gradually (and not so gradually!) reshaped by humans into houses, shopping malls, asphalt parking lots, skyscrapers, bike lanes, and freeways, birds are being forced to try to adapt and survive in this giant man-made wilderness. So when a big flock of robins happens, by chance, to find a real live tree, we should forgive them for losing control in all the excitement.

It's Party Time!

Crisp mornings and falling-down-drunk birds, intoxicated with fermented pyracantha berries, are a sure sign that fall is finally here. Only the birds aren't really drunk and the berries aren't really fermented.

Nevertheless, sometime every fall, flocks of robins migrate to warmer climates to escape winter temperatures, and Bay Area gardens have become popular pit stops along the way for birds who need to refuel. The starving birds usually lay over a week or so to dine on tasty berries, worms, and other tidbits before continuing their journey south.

That's when we humans first notice something is amiss—when bleary-eyed robins start banging against our windows to be let in or standing around singing in little groups on street corners.

"Don't step on them, Agnes, they're drunk!"

"That's disgusting!"

And, of course, the electronic and print media will have a field day. Photographers can show viewers a gutter's-eye view of the seamy side of bird life as we columnists toss off choice little anthropomorphic witticisms about the "feathery little deadbeats."

Well, what are we supposed to think, for crying out loud? They look drunk. They stagger. They bump into objects. They fly low and with great difficulty, making them easy targets for cars. And they have been sighted burping up berries in the gutter.

And if they look drunk, then those fuzzy little lushes, I mean thrushes, must be drunk, right?

Wrong! In reality, the birds are just suffering the aftereffects of a serious case of overeating. You know how you feel when you get up from the Thanksgiving dinner table after your annual attempt to eat yourself to death? You stagger around and bump into things. Maybe you even burp up a few cranberries. This is not unlike what happens to the robins. When they land in your yard, they are starving, and they dive headlong into the berry bushes in a feeding frenzy made all the more frantic by each other's competitive actions as they fight to see who can consume the most berries in a single gulp. Bird life is further complicated when blood sugar levels, suddenly elevated from gorging on those sweet berries, contribute to the avian hyperactivity.

All this compulsive overeating also results in top-heavy, overweight birds who stagger around the sky as they try to deal with the effects of gravity on dramatically modified flight characteristics. Filled to the brim with ten to fifteen juicy berries apiece—about a fifth of each bird's natural weight—they are no longer graceful fliers. They plow into walls and windows and nosedive into the streets.

They're out of it, all right, but it has nothing to do with alcohol. In fact, those fresh, unfermented, non-alcoholic berries are a prime source of nutritious food for many wild creatures. The pyracantha berry is the potato of the bird world. Opossums, foxes, and raccoons also enjoy stuffing their faces with berries like kids dipping into a jam jar. Squirrels eat them like apples.

As the bushes burst forth in our spring gardens and berries start the long ripening process throughout summer and into fall, it takes only a few rains and a couple of frosts to bring the sugar content of those tiny "apples" to the point where wild creatures start to take notice. This ripening process will continue from approximately October through January, depending on the subspecies of berry, air temperature, available moisture, and other environmental factors.

It is quite obvious that birds can tell the difference in flavor between ripe and unripe berries. I've seen whole flocks of robins skip over entire bushes because the berries obviously didn't taste just right to them. It's Mother Nature's way, you know. They shall eat no berry before its time.

Sparrows ....

Golden-crowned sparrow (*Zonotrichia atricapilla*); white-crowned sparrow (*Zonotrichia leucophrys*)

These are just two of the familiar sparrow species you might see hopping around in your backyard. Both of these little brown birds feed primarily on seeds, buds, grass, flower petals, fruit, and insects. I often spot golden-crowned sparrows at my seed feeders and on the ground (they look like rocks moving), but the white-crowned sparrows are solely ground-feeders, usually in the thick bushes where the Cooper's hawk won't spot them when she makes her morning flyover.

You can always tell it's winter when you look out the window and see lots of white-crowned and golden-crowned heads bobbing up and down under the bushes in your backyard. The rest of those brown sparrow bodies are so camouflaged against the damp earth and leaves that it's almost impossible to see them, other than having a vague impression that the ground is moving.

These winter sparrows move around your yard like flocks of little vacuum cleaners. One year my wife and I had just finished planting about a dozen nice, big, leafy red-leaf lettuce plants in our garden box on a Saturday morning. That afternoon the sparrows arrived. On Sunday there was nothing left of our beautiful lettuce plants but one-inch tall green stubs. Later, observation of these always hungry birds in action showed that each bird would bite off a large piece of lettuce leaf in its beak and gobble it down as it hopped past the plant.

"Welcome to our yard," I called out the back door. "Enjoy the lettuce we planted for you!" White-crowned and golden-crowned sparrows are the most aggressive ground-feeders I have ever seen. Period.

Drop That Peanut!

The two scrub jays that live in my backyard (the Blue Brothers) aren't too sure they like the idea of migrating songbirds visiting their territory. The other morning, the jays landed on our deck and started squawking for their breakfast peanuts, so I tossed a couple out for their treat. But before either of the Blue Brothers could lift a feather, a white-crowned sparrow and a golden-crowned sparrow zoomed down out of nowhere to snatch up the peanuts and disappear into the nearby bushes.

As the confused scrub jays hopped around in circles on the deck, looking for their peanuts, my indoor cats, Tut and Hello Newman, rolled

around on the floor just inside the sliding glass door, laughing and snickering hysterically. As you might guess, they really hate those jays, but they sure do like those two sparrows!

Starlings ....

European starling (*Sturnus vulgaris*)

A local rancher once wrote me about a problem he was having with European starlings in the expansive backyard of his ranch:

> They migrate through by the millions in the fall. They invade our orchards and vineyards and do extensive damage to our crops. Many stay through the winter in our hills to consume the insects and fruits necessary to support our native birds; and they take over their breeding cavities in the old trees.

He claimed that on his ranch, kestrels and acorn woodpeckers had not been able to raise any young for the last three years. In the winter, the starlings would start driving away the kestrels and woodpeckers by incessant harassment, physical and verbal. They also monopolized the food source, consuming the insects needed by thrashers, towhees, bluebirds, nuthatches, titmice, tanagers, red-winged blackbirds, wrens, quail, and many others. The rancher had tried everything to prevent this, but the starlings just kept coming in ever larger numbers.

He proposed a "practical solution" that would control this starling infestation, saying he would need the cooperation of all the nearby wineries, the local environmentalists, of course, and the state Fish and Game Department. His idea was that, as the starling flocks started coming in the fall as "vast black clouds," skeet shooters hidden in blinds in the vineyards would hunt them. Then "four and twenty blackbirds would be baked in a pie and served up during our Wine Festival." The rancher claimed that after a few years, even though the starlings would always remain a threat, the ecological balance would be fully restored, allowing native birds to regain their former numbers.

Blasting away at those "vast black clouds" would undoubtedly kill thousands of birds, but in the greater scheme of things, this carnage would be an utter, and immoral, waste. There are far too many millions of starlings in this country for the deaths of even a few hundred thousand birds to have any ecological effect. The dead starlings would just be bloody drops in the bucket.

And you can forget about restoring any ecological balance. After more than a hundred years since forty European starlings were supposedly imported and first released in New York City's Central Park in 1890, starlings have long ago been established as a permanent part of that mythical ecological balance.

It's incredibly easy for us humans to screw up the environment. Fixing it is a wee bit more complicated than gorging on blackbird pie.

Woodpeckers ....

Acorn woodpecker
(Melanerpes formicivorus)

This red-headed character is a real circus clown as it noisily scurries up and down and around trees, hunting for sweet sap, fruit, and insects to eat. The acorn woodpecker drills deep holes in dead branches and telephone poles (hey, they're wood, aren't they?) with its chisel-like beak and stuffs the holes with acorns so it can eat them in winter. Acorn moths will also lay eggs in the acorns, and when the woodpeckers get around to feasting on their stash, they will often find the acorn moth larvae adds a tasty source of protein to their diets.

A very thick skull keeps this bird from getting a headache during all that pecking.

Drop That Acorn or I'll Stuff You in a Hole in a Telephone Pole!

Once I was scheduled to do a television program about woodpeckers, so I paid a visit to the Lindsay Wildlife Museum and got permission to use a non-releasable acorn woodpecker to go on the show with me. (The woodpecker had been orphaned and hand-raised by a local resident and completely tamed and imprinted in the process. The bird finally made its way to the museum's wildlife rescue program but by that time it was too tame to return to the wild. The museum often uses non-releasable wildlife like this for educational purposes.)

While I was doing the live TV program with that little red-headed nut, I was explaining how acorn woodpeckers drill holes in branches and telephone poles to store acorns for the winter. I was demonstrating my talk with a three-foot piece of power pole riddled with woodpecker holes that were stuffed full of acorns. As I pulled out an acorn to show how tightly they fit into the perfect-size holes, the woodpecker, who had been clinging quietly to my shoulder, let out a primal scream of mortal pain, dove down to my hand, yanked the acorn out of my fingers and shoved it back down into its hole in the power pole. Sheesh! Don't *ever* mess with an acorn woodpecker's acorns!

Northern flicker (Colaptes auratus)

One winter I spotted two male flickers chasing each other and flying from branch to branch in the trees in my backyard. They landed on opposite sides of my plum tree, scooted around on the bark a bit, and then took off again to chase each other.

Why all the aggressive action between those two male birds? It seemed obvious: I figured it was all a matter of turf. One male flicker felt my yard was in his territory and the other male was obviously intruding. That's how these little jousts sometimes happen, and they're rarely planned. So there doesn't always have to be a female bird around to set things off, but one may have been demurely observing the duel from a nearby tree.

How to Be a Good Woodpecker Neighbor

Got a problem with a woodpecker trying to poke holes in your roof or the side of your house? Most likely the woodpecker needs a hole so it will have a warm place to sleep at night. If you hang a 10" x 10" wooden birdhouse nearby (it should have a two-inch entrance hole about five inches above the floor), it might quiet things down. You can either make the woodpecker house yourself out of rough-cut wood (so it's easier for the woodpecker to get a grip and hang onto it), or you can usually pick one up from a nearby bird specialty store.

Miscellaneous Birds ....

House (English) sparrow (*Passer domesticus*); California towhee (*Pipilo crissalis*); dark-eyed (Oregon) junco (*Junco hyemalis*)

I stood at my family room window sipping hot coffee from the biggest cup I could find and staring out into the cold, gray, and very wet dawn. Just a few feet away on the other, wetter side of the window glass, a soggy little house sparrow hung on for dear life to the wooden feeder perch as the wind swung the bird feeder violently back and forth—a silent wind chime with a broken clapper.

On the cement patio under the feeder, a California towhee and an Oregon junco crouched next to each other, each of them occasionally bending down to peck at one of the seeds that had been tossed from the crazily swinging perch above them.

All three birds had something in common: a steady stream of water was trickling down their backs—a trio of little creeks that had overflowed their banks—and was dripping off the ends of their feathers. It had been raining and blowing steadily all night.

Then there was an abrupt lull in the storm and the sparrow stretched up straight, fluffed into a huge ball, shook its body violently, flinging water all over the outside of the window, and instantly became a sleek, dry bird standing tall and ready for action. Below him on the wet cement, the towhee and the junco had also done the same. They all looked like new birds. Amazing.

The mechanical structure of bird feathers was designed by centuries of evolution to create a warm, waterproof covering around the bird. A quick shake by the wearer instantly removes all traces of water. Unlike the wet hairs on the sodden gray cat that was huddled under the drooping redwood branches on the other side of the yard, the steady drip-drip-drip from the redwood needles landed on top of its head, creating puddle craters in the long fur. As the sopping kitty stood up to leave, he gave several mighty shakes in a frustrating attempt to dislodge all the moisture and finally gave up and just stood there dripping water into a rapidly forming puddle like a wet sponge that somebody forgot to squeeze out. There was more water dripping onto his body than there was dripping off. It was definitely a losing battle. He finally slunk off into the bushes, heading home to shake water all over the couch and dry off. His human would not be a happy trooper.

The sparrow meanwhile gave a bright "chirp!" and continued to crack the tiny seed shells with the sharp sides of its beak and swallow the tasty insides. I heard a similar "peep!" from the towhee.

Suddenly, the sky overflowed with a gush of water and wind that enveloped my yard and made everything disappear in a gigantic gray and white SPLASH! After it all slowly drained away, the sparrow, towhee, and junco were gone.

Oak (plain) titmouse (Parus inornatus); bushtit (Psaltriparus minimus); chestnut-backed chickadee (Parus rufescens); rock dove (pigeon) (Columbia livia); band-tailed pigeon (Columbia fasciata); ad infinitum

See that small gray acrobat with a feathered crest, swinging from twigs and constantly poking around in cracks for spiders and other things to eat? Titmice are another good reason (besides the fact that it's also a fun family project!) to build birdhouses because these little birds will line up

to nest in them. Titmice forage for seeds and insects and spiders and like to stop by your feeders for an occasional snack when other birds aren't around, because they're kind of shy.

The other gray birds, a little bit larger than a hummingbird, are the ones you always hear in your yard but never see. Bushtit flocks flit invisibly through your trees looking for insects crawling on the leaves and bark. They build their nests out of spiderwebs and plants, making them look like little hanging socks. Female bushtits have yellow eyes and the males' eyes are dark brown. Now I challenge you to get close enough to see if that's true.

"Rock dove" is just another fancy name for a pigeon. These incredibly adaptable birds seem to do best when they are around humans. This is probably why rock doves may be one of the world's oldest domesticated bird species (since around 4000 B.C. or so). Because of their extremely messy habits (ahem, by human standards) and the fact that they tend to congregate in large flocks and create huge quantities of poop under where they perch, the pigeon is not a particularly popular backyard bird. But then you knew that, didn't you?

You never know what you're going to see at your bird feeders or flying around in your yard. Chickadees are groping through the holes in your feeders, looking for black-oil sunflower seeds, and the wilder and bigger band-tailed pigeons occasionally come circling over your yard as you run out frantically waving your arms and yelling "NO! NO! NO!" as you try to keep them from landing and becoming permanent fixtures on your roof.

Nobody's perfect, not even some of your wild bird neighbors.

How to Be a Good Songbird Neighbor

Keep Your Feeders Clean

Would you serve your dinner guests food on cracked or dirty plates? Of course you wouldn't. So why would you do that to the wild birds that visit or live in your yard? Dirty bird feeders spread disease, so it's important for you to always keep your bird feeders fresh and clean. It only takes about twenty-five minutes of your time, once a week, to wash your bird feeders with soap and water and then soak them for ten minutes in a mild bleach solution (one-quarter cup of bleach to one quart of water). This will kill all bacteria and many viruses.

It's better if you don't wash your feeders in your kitchen sink. Salmonella occurs naturally in most wild bird populations, and even healthy birds are often carriers of this bacteria, which is transmitted through their droppings. I wash my feeders in a bucket, and when I'm through, I sterilize the bucket and my hands with the bleach mix.

Before washing your feeders, be sure to remove all the old seed that is caked on and sticking to the insides, especially that mysterious black gunk that sometimes appears on the inside bottom of a feeder. This is especially important in winter, when seed gets wet and harbors fungus and mold. Wet seed, by the way, should be changed immediately and replaced with dry seed. It only takes a day for mold to form on wet seed. (Shame on you if you ever discover green grass blades growing in the bottom of your feeder!)

Bird Feeding Tips

- Keep the area under your seed feeders clean. Remove as much spilled seed as possible. Dig it out of cracks and toss it in the garbage.
- If it still looks bad on the ground under your feeder, spray it with some of the bleach solution you used to clean your feeder. Spray the area just before dark, after birds and pets retire. The bleach will break down into harmless components by morning. Bleach is a fungicide and bactericide and also kills a lot of viruses.
- Don't use a feeder that lets birds stand around in the seed mix and contaminate it with their feces. This can spread disease.
- Migratory birds from all over the country pass through the San Francisco Bay Area as they head north, south, east, west, or wherever their eternal quest for warm weather and more food takes them. These wild birds are always a colorful sight in your yard, but they can sometimes carry invisible bacteria and viruses that can be passed along to the other birds that use your feeders. If you notice any sick birds (usually fluffed up and quiet compared to other birds in the flock) it's probably a good idea to take down your feeders for a couple of days to let the birds disperse and to prevent healthy birds from coming into contact with the sick ones.
- Don't forget that hummingbirds absolutely hate the taste of chlorine! After washing your hummer feeders out with the bleach solution, you might want to wash them again with some soap and hot water. Then dry them in the sun (if you can find any), refill them with fresh nectar, and stand back!

Your Garage Can Be Dangerous to Birds

For some reason birds, especially hummingbirds, buzz into a lot of garages. They fly up into the rafters and won't come back down and fly out of the garage. For hummingbirds, who need to eat every fifteen minutes or so, that's a problem. So why won't they fly back out of the garage?

All birds instinctively fly *up* when they're in trouble. That's why they don't want to fly back *down* and out through the open garage door when they get trapped inside. That means when any bird accidentally flies into your garage you need to do something to tempt them to leave.

If you have a hummingbird feeder, hang it low to the ground (on a long string) in plain view in front of the open door. This might help to attract the hungry bird down to where it can see back out into the real world...and freedom. Hummingbirds are easiest to tempt because they are very attracted to anything red. That's why they feed on red, pink, and purple flowers. Put as many different red things as you can find on the ground just inside and outside the open garage door: red cloth, red flowers, red paper, etc. Then back off so you won't frighten the bird and keep it up in the rafters. Once, to get a hummingbird down from high inside the steeple area of a huge church and out through the open doors, I spread a red tablecloth on the floor.

On rare occasions, trapped songbirds are able to work things out for themselves with a little help from their friends, who are sometime chirping in a tree just outside the garage door. But if nothing works, you may need to throw a bath towel over the bird, catch it, and release it yourself.

Wild creatures that live in the city need to develop a whole new set of behaviors to help them cope with the manmade environment. Birds that instinctively fly up and away to get out of trouble need to modify that escape response and learn to fly down and out through doors and windows when they get trapped in buildings. It's happening, albeit slowly, but then Mother Nature has a mind of her own and never was one to move fast or make snap decisions. It'll happen.

Gulls, Ravens, and Crows

Ring-billed gull *(Larus delawarensis)*; California gull *(Larus californicus)*

Gulls are the ultimate scroungers. That's why you'll find a gull sitting on top of just about every light pole in sight when you visit a local shopping center or mall. These parking lots are perfect places to look for food that has been dropped or carelessly tossed aside by us messy humans. The gulls know that.

Common raven *(Corvus corax)*; American crow *(Corvus brachyrhynchos)*

Ever wondered what the basic difference is between a crow and a raven? The common raven stands about two feet tall. Its huge head, enormous beak, and a scruff of unkempt feathers on its neck give it a chunky, tough-guy look. A guttural "gronk, gronk" adds to the effect. The shorter and more slender American crow stands one to one-and-a-half feet tall and has a smaller head, a slender beak, and goes "caw, caw, caw."

What has caused crows to so suddenly appear in urban and suburban communities throughout the San Francisco Bay Area? While it may look like they appeared suddenly, they've actually been gradually popping up in towns and cities around the San Francisco Bay in larger and larger numbers for the past ten to twenty years. A classic example is the shopping center where I forage for my groceries in Benicia. I used to park in the lot and see a gull atop every light pole.

Sometime around 1990, the number of crows in Benicia started to increase, and I'd see them standing on poles with the gulls, or instead of the gulls. Today, the crows are everywhere in Benicia—flocks of ten to twenty tall black shadows pecking on the ground in open space areas between the houses or sitting like big black candles in somebody's tree. I've also started to see a few ravens, and I suspect the same thing is happening with them, only it's probably a little more obvious in coastal communities where they are more common.

It used to be that if you wanted to see a crow you'd have to head for farming areas and the fields and woodlands around Eastern Contra Costa County (Brentwood), or south to the farms and ranches and fields of Pleasanton and Livermore, or north or south along the coastline.

There's been a lot of development in many areas where the crows and ravens lived, causing these birds to find themselves gradually surrounded by ever growing suburban areas. Being scavengers, the big black birds thrive on the unlimited amount of garbage and other foods in the malls and residential areas. We humans really make it easy for them to like to live next door to us.

As more and more crows and ravens start to nest and raise families in closer proximity to us, we're finally starting to notice the population increase. They've actually been around for a long time, but when a big flock drops by to visit your own neighborhood, filling your backyard with their noisy "caw, caw, cawing," it sure seems like they've appeared suddenly.

Game Birds, Shorebirds, and Waterfowl

Game Birds ....

Ring-necked pheasant *(Phasianus colchicus)*

These large, long-tailed, rooster-like Asian birds were introduced into North America in the 1850s so we humans could run around with our shotguns and dogs and hunt them. They are now just about everywhere, including Hawaii. You can't miss the cock pheasant's springtime "gronk! gronk! gronk!" echoing across the fields. And in the fall, when the grass gets dry and turns brown, pheasants occasionally visit our suburban yards in search of good things to eat, especially those tasty things growing in your garden.

There are a lot of ring-necked pheasants living in open space around the San Francisco Bay Area, and occasionally some will get their signals crossed and wander into yards or downtown streets. If they're lucky, they'll meet a nice animal control officer who will help them find their way back home. We can only expect to have more wild encounters in the future, as new homes and shopping centers continue to carve up the environment into a latticework of homes and shopping centers.

Sometimes these encounters are benign, sometimes not, and sometimes they're just annoying. One family whose home in the East Bay suburbs backs up against an open space reported they'd had a pheasant living in their yard off and on for seven years and had even seen him once in a while with a "harem" of lady pheasants. Things started to go downhill when he took to sitting on the roof of their front porch and pecking at an upstairs window. This was bad enough for the people, but it was driving their standard poodle crazy—they were afraid he'd go through the window. I suggested that they put some sort of cover on the outside of their fancy "mirror" so the cock pheasant wouldn't be able to see that other handsome fellow who was hanging around, trying to steal his girlfriends.

The other day, a caller reported a pheasant standing on a busy downtown street corner in the small Bay Area city of Richmond, waiting for the light to change. When the light finally turned green, the pheasant looked both ways before starting across the street. I think they are starting to adapt to living with humans.

California quail (*Callipepla californica*)

A woman who lives near that roof-dwelling pheasant found herself stopped in traffic on her way home recently as seven tiny quail babies followed their mom across the street. The mom and dad jumped up on the curb, she said, but the babies were so small the wind kept blowing them over. They were obviously too tiny to get up on the curb, but they kept trying, to the point of exhaustion, while their mother called to them. Hesitant to intervene, my reader finally decided to help and gently picked up each baby (the mother, very excited, was now screaming) and placed it on the sidewalk. And then, one by one, the babies followed their parents up the hillside and crept under their mother's protective wings.

It's often pretty hard for the smaller wild residents of our suburban wilderness to negotiate their way around our artificial environment. In this case, the quail parents might have been able to figure something out eventually, or the babies might have strayed down the gutter and fallen into a culvert—it happens with ducklings all the time. Normally, I'm a believer in nonintervention. But I've also learned over the years that there are exceptions to most rules. You just have to evaluate the situation and take your best shot at dealing with it. In this case, I probably would have helped those baby quail to the top of the curb, too. Sometimes it is okay to fool with Mother Nature.

One reader with a small putting green in his front yard noticed that the normally lush and brilliant green grass was beginning to disappear and there were little holes in the resulting bare ground. Then he noticed a family of quail in his front yard. He and his wife stood by the window and watched as six adult quail and six chicks ruthlessly pulled up the remaining bent grass (a durable grass designed for commercial golf greens that keeps its density and fine texture while being mown very low). They continued for some time until the mail truck arrived to send them scurrying.

Everyone loves quail. I get mail all the time from people who want to know how to attract quail to their yards. Now here's someone with his own little personal covey of beautiful California quail and they're eating up his putting green. Life is tough.

Quail eat the bent grass and scratch in the soil underneath as they forage for seeds and insects. I offered what I hope was a win-win solution. Plant nurseries sell plastic owls for use in scaring birds away from gardens. I suggested placing one of those owls in the middle of the putting green and then scattering bird seed in an open spot in the backyard to attract the quail there. Putting around the owl probably added a stroke or two to the man's golf score, but that seems like a fair trade-off to me.

Wild turkey *(Meleagris gallopavo)*

We know that wild turkeys used to gobble in California ten thousand or so years ago because turkey bones have been found in the La Brea tar pits in Los Angeles. But they were also brought to the state in small numbers over the years: a few were introduced about 1908 for hunting, sixty were transplanted from Texas to San Diego in 1959, and a flock of thirty was released in Santa Clara in 1978. At present, the combined efforts of the National Wild Turkey Federation (a hunters' organization) and the California Department of Fish and Game have boosted the state's wild turkey numbers to more than one hundred thousand, and there are more and more every spring after nesting season.

Wild turkeys normally live in the undeveloped Sierra Nevada foothills, foraging for acorns, plants, seeds, and insects. They nest in poison oak and tall grass to hide from bobcats and coyotes and roost at night in the relative safety of oak trees. But venturing into suburban yards, they have found lots of good things to eat, and now there is a wild turkey population explosion in the East Bay suburbs.

Residents of Livermore and Pleasanton, just south and east of the San Francisco Bay, started seeing these eighteen- to thirty-five-pound gobblers in their yards in the early 1990s. Small flocks soon wandered into Danville, around the slopes of Mount Diablo, and into populated areas of Walnut Creek, a few miles north. Around February 2001, a reader in nearby Lafayette sent me a picture of forty wild turkeys gobbling up a storm on her front lawn. The following December, I started to hear about small flocks a few miles away, in Moraga and Orinda. I suspected the large Lafayette flock had started to split into smaller ones. The big birds were soon wandering down the middle of main thoroughfares, backing up delighted and not-so-delighted drivers during the morning commute.

Wild turkey flocks are usually made up of a male gobbler and some hens. "Some" can mean anything from two to more than thirty. They eat acorns, seeds, insects, and whole gardens, which tends to complicate relationships among human neighbors—when one neighbor feeds the turkeys store-bought grain every day, another feeds the turkeys whether he or she likes it or not.

I don't know how smart wild turkeys are, but they are instinctive experts when it comes to foraging for food and hiding from hunters. They can spot the blink of a hunter's eye at a hundred feet and fly away fast, at fifty miles an hour. Now that they're starting to move into town with us humans and our human conveyances, I just hope they remember to look both ways before crossing the busy streets.

A woman wrote me that she shooed a wild turkey out of busy traffic in Pinole, a small town that has seen rapid development recently. She said the big gobbler was in the middle of the road, squawking, as cars maneuvered around him. "I chased him up a side road to a park," she said. "He screamed in outrage the entire length of our inter-action and was still yelling when I drove away."

An outraged turkey blocking traffic? The morning commute is finally starting to gobble us all up. Arrgghh!

I have a friend who tries to hunt wild turkeys every spring. He dresses himself from head to toe in state-of-the-art Navy Seal camouflage gear, smears his face and hands with a curiously mot-tled gray, black, and olive camouflage paint, wraps his fancy shotgun with dull green netting so the metal barrel and highly buffed wooden stock can't reflect sunlight, and heads for the woods. If he sits down on the lawn to tie his boot string on the way to his truck, he disappears.

For as long as I've known about his little obsession, my friend has never even seen a wild turkey, let alone shot one. If you hear a loud, ago-nizing scream in the distance, that's him reading what I wrote above about wild turkeys standing around in people's front yards.

Shorebirds ....

Snowy egret (Egretta thula); great egret (Ardea alba)

A lot of backyard fish fanciers have been shocked more than once to discover herons dabbling their beaks in their fancy fishponds. I know one koi col-lector who lost $20,000 worth (his figure) of fancy koi one summer to egrets and herons.

I got a request for help from one couple whose fishponds had been untouched for eighteen years before they started noticing their fish disappear-ing. They had spotted an egret sitting on their fence and immediately staked a large nylon gar-den net over the ponds; they wanted to know if I thought it would work.

They were in shock at having their ponds dis-covered after all those years, especially since the ponds were partially hidden under a tree and shade cloth, but some egrets and herons can actually become quite skilled at spotting backyard "fishing holes." My guess is that this character was flying by at a low altitude and spotted a reflection off the pool surfaces. Egrets are very good at doing that.

I thought their idea to stretch a garden net over the ponds would work fine. I also suggested that they go to a garden supply store and pick up three or four of those plastic great horned owls and perch them here and there on poles around the pond area. Scare owls don't fool a lot of ani-mals, but they seem to work pretty well at fright-ening off egrets and herons. I told the couple to make sure they regularly moved the owls around to different positions to make the egret think they were real. And remember: You can fool all of the egrets some of the time, and some of the egrets all of the time—but you can't fool all of the egrets all of the time. (That little ditty was supposedly composed by a goldfish named Fred who used to live in a backyard pond until he flew off one day.)

Great blue heron (Ardea herodias); green heron (Butorides virescens)

A woman and her husband were strolling through a little marina on the edge of San Francisco Bay one sunny afternoon when they witnessed a small great blue heron catching a very big gopher on one of the lawns. The e-mail message described how the heron stood quietly for a few minutes, as if contemplating what to do with the enormous gopher. The gangly bird finally flew to the edge of the bay, just a short distance away, and started dunking the gopher into the water. She said her husband thought the heron was trying to drown the gopher, while she figured it was just trying to make the rodent easier to swallow.

I wrote her back and told her I also thought water was an excellent lubricant and wet gophers go down easier than dry ones. (In case you're wondering, I learned that from observation, not practice.) Green and great blue herons normally prey on gophers, mice, snakes, lizards, frogs, toads, and small birds, in addition to all those fish they catch.

An Old Gladiator

Spring is an energizing time to get lost along Mendocino's rugged coastline. Mostly my wife and I go there to just read books and take long walks.

The huge, old great blue heron was still standing in the same meadow where we met him when we got lost there three years ago. He let me pass within five feet of him. His head came up to my chest, and his beak reminded me of one of those brutal Roman short swords favored by gladiators for gutting their opponents. Look out Western toads and fence lizards!

We met Mother Nature while we were there. She hasn't changed much since I last saw her. Some gray hair, but I think it's genetic and she inherited it from her dad. She looks so young

and beautiful in the spring with those flowers in her hair.

Waterfowl ....

Every community pond in a suburban or urban community has a never-ending supply of geese and ducks. Even the smallest body of water in the middle of a human-populated area is a powerful magnetic attraction to these big waterfowl. They need a place—any place—to paddle around and forage for food. A small natural pond in the middle of a park or a huge cement lake in the middle of a busy city—they'll take what they can get.

The waterfowl arrive from all directions and have become a huge management problem. Wild Canada geese come "honk, honk, honking" and mallards come "quack, quack, quacking" down out of the skies every fall during migration time, and a few of them always decide to stick around and fraternize with the domestics when the majority of the flock heads back north in the springtime.

About a week or two every Easter, hundreds, maybe thousands, of fuzzy little goslings and ducklings also get dropped off at these ponds and lakes when parents decide they've had enough of these Easter pets. And a steady stream of other pet geese get dropped off in the night to add to the growing din.

The end result is too many geese and ducks. And too much goose and duck poop. And not enough food. And you can't believe the terror in a small boy's eyes when mommy takes him down to feed the geese and the geese, all bigger than he is, come charging over in a thunderous, honking herd to knock him flat on his back and start pecking and trying to gobble him up. It is the stuff of nightmares.

"But Mommy, there *is* something under my bed...a big mean goose!"

Mallard (*Anas platyrhynchos*); Pekin duck (white domestic) (*Anas domesticus*)

The mallard duck and the Pekin duck are two of the most common ducks to be found paddling around the community ponds and lakes in the East Bay. Mallards have become a particular problem in the last decade. Flying back and forth from isolated pond to isolated lake, they have started spotting tiny bodies of water called "swimming pools" in people's backyards. Every spring, I am inundated with e-mail messages and letters and phone calls from East Bay residents who have discovered ducks paddling around their swimming pools and nesting in their roses. The ducks think it's great having their own private ponds, but the humans are aghast at the amount of duck poop clogging their swimming pool filters.

Alas, in the rush of things, ducks and humans alike tend to forget about the tiny, newly hatched ducklings. As a rule, these little fuzzy creatures will suffer a 100 percent mortality rate as they are rapidly consumed by house cats, raccoons, opossums, skunks, family dogs, scrub jays, and great horned owls at night. That is assuming that some of them will be able to climb out over the high sides of the swimming pools without drowning.

Canada goose (*Branta canadensis*)

A riddle: A Canada goose is nesting on a warehouse roof over a dumpster. It is almost time for the eggs to hatch and the roof is ten feet above the ground. How will the goslings get off the roof safely?

Canada geese sometimes nest in trees and on cliffs. When it's time for the babies to learn to fly, the mother goose usually flies down to the ground first and starts calling back up for her chicks to come to mama. The chicks respond by jumping off the rooftop, tree, or cliff, one at a time, like little tennis balls, all that fuzz cushioning their landing.

How to Be a Good Goose and Duck Neighbor

Don't feed them bread. Hungry geese and ducks will frantically gobble up whole pieces of bread, which overwhelms their system. I've seen people dump whole grocery bags full of old, dried bread on the side of a local pond and it disappeared in seconds as a charging herd of geese and ducks arrived to devour the stuff.

Before the bread can be transferred to the stomach and digested, it is held temporarily in the bird's crop. While the bread is in the crop, the bird drinks a lot of water and the bread turns into a plaster-like substance and hardens. I once saw a big Canada goose brought into a wildlife rescue center because it had such a big lump of hardened bread stuck in its crop that it couldn't eat or drink. It was near death. The cement-solid bread had to be removed by a veterinary surgeon.

If you're going to feed the geese, use chicken scratch and other grains from a feed store. They also like produce, grapes, and garden snails. Leave the bread home in the garbage can where you were planning to toss it in the first place before someone said, "Let's go feed it to the geese."

Toulouse goose (domestic) (*Anser anser*); Chinese goose (white domestic) (*Anser cygnoides*)

The big gray Toulouse goose and the smaller white Chinese goose are the most common geese to be found at most community ponds in the East Bay. A band of former pets, they wander around like lost children—street geese—begging for food from anyone who will listen.

Horned grebe (*Podiceps auritus*)

During winter in the rainy season, these little grebes will sometimes land on shiny wet roads, thinking they are creeks or rivers. The design of these aquatic birds, with feet at the rear of the body for more-efficient paddling, makes it very difficult for them to stand. They also usually need a running (swimming?) start to take off from the water, so after landing on the hard pavement they're usually grounded. These grebes are sometimes "rescued" and taken to local wildlife centers for care. If no injuries are found, the birds are taken to a pond or lake closest to where they were recovered and placed in the water so they can take off. They usually do so, immediately.

If you find such a grounded grebe and have no wildlife center to care for it, try releasing it yourself in a nearby lake or pond. Just drop a towel gently over the bird (they can bite!) and carefully place it in a cardboard box or large brown paper grocery sack for transportation.

Raptors

Hawks, falcons, owls, vultures, and eagles are among the most powerful, graceful, and skillful fliers in the bird world. Many of the great birds have adapted well to living in close proximity to humans, and our buildings offer some of the hawks, falcons, and owls good places to build their nests. Some of them will even hunt in our yards, while the more wary birds of prey will circle high above us every day, checking out the strange two-legged creatures who have remodeled their world.

Backyard Hunting

We have a bench in a corner of our backyard by our little grove of three redwood trees. It's a quiet room sheltered on three sides by the thirty-foot redwoods, a large ceanothus bush, and a twenty-foot apple tree. The redwood branches grow down the trunks to the ground in a green wall. I like to sit there and listen to the wind or the singing of the birds or just lean back and stare up at the blue ceiling and get hypnotized by the swaying of the trees as the world passes me by.

One Sunday morning I was listening to the wild birds when it suddenly got very quiet. One minute the air was full of song and then-nothing. It was crazy. Birds don't instantly decide to stop singing all at once on the count of three. Unless...

The sound of large wings flapping somewhere in the depths of the redwood trees—slap-slap-slapping against the branches—the crash of a large body through brittle twigs—moving fast—it was too purposeful. A hawk! Maybe a sharp-shinned hawk or a Cooper's hawk. A bird hunter. I froze in the position I was in so I wouldn't disturb the action and waited to see what would happen next.

Songbirds are so fearful of these predators that the mere shadow of the bird passing across the ground is like a magic wand that causes all bird songs to instantly cease as sparrows dive into bushes and juncos scuttle under the deck and fat mourning doves press into the ground and hope they look like rocks. ·

The crashing stopped. I strained to listen. Nothing.

Then, just the hint of a rustle by the ground. And an instant later something big heard it too and crashed down to that spot. I could follow them by the sounds. Something was stalking a small bird in the dark forest of my redwood trees. An even louder CRASH! A sudden, softer scurrying sound. Another CRASH! More scurrying. Silence. Another miss.

A male junco darted from the redwoods, zipped under my legs, and dove headlong into the soft, fuzzy depths of the potted geranium by my bench.

Another CRASH! under the redwoods.

A white-crowned sparrow dashed along the ground out from under the trees and into my wife's potted orchid jungle. I couldn't help feeling a little shiver down the back of my neck as I had a mental picture of something large and hairy lunging out at me through the waving redwood branches.

Whatever the hawk was chasing suddenly seemed to panic. Lots of rustling and scurrying sounds—the flit, flit, flit of wings brushing the branches, the CRASH! CRASH! CRASH! of the predator as it followed close behind. I caught a flash of blue in the green. Maybe a scrub jay. More silence.

I sat there unmoving for another ten minutes without hearing another sound. And then all of a sudden I realized there was a Cooper's hawk sitting in the apple tree, her fierce, red eyes staring down into my own!

She must have sensed I was there and had stopped chasing the jay to stalk silently from the redwoods like a ghost to check me out. I don't know how long she had been watching me, but she turned without warning, spread her wings wide, and glided through the apple tree branches and over the back fence and down across the little canyon behind my house toward the eucalyptus tree where she built her nest last spring.

I could hear her calling, "Kac-kac-kac-kac!" I wonder what she meant by that?

Owls...

Barn owl *(Tyto alba)*

At three weeks of age, a barn owl chick is growing and developing so rapidly it needs to consume about eight mice or two gophers a night. If there are six barn owl chicks in one nest (the average), that means the two parent owls will need to hunt and kill up to forty-eight mice or twelve gophers (or the equivalent in Jerusalem crickets, rats, bats, etc.) *every* night to keep their always ravenous youngsters healthy and growing. That's why gardeners are delighted when a pair of barn owls decides to nest in the hollow of a nearby tree.

I get a lot of mail from cat owners who want to know if barn owls prey on felines. They particularly want to know if these owls can pick up an animal as large as a ten- to fifteen-pound cat. The answer to that is don't worry about barn owls and your cat. These medium-size owls prey on mice, gophers, and other small rodents, usually swallowing them in one quick gulp. A two-pound barn owl can barely take off with a full-grown gopher, let alone a fifteen-pound cat. I don't even think a twelve-pound adult female golden eagle could lift a fifteen-pound cat off the ground (although the eagle would probably still kill the cat).

Another common owl question has to do with what appears to be digested balls of fur, a little bigger than a large walnut, containing bones and teeth that you might find at the base of a tree in your yard.

When owls catch rodents and swallow them whole, the parts of their prey that can't be digested—usually fur, skeleton, tiny wrist watches—are regurgitated as those walnut-size packages ("owl pellets") of fur and bone. If you take tweezers and carefully pull one of those pellets apart, you can sometimes find the whole skeleton of a mouse or gopher. This will give you a good idea what the owls in your neighborhood are feeding on. I once found a pellet that was nothing but the indigestible remains of fifteen to twenty Jerusalem crickets that a barn owl had gobbled up one night.

Burrowing owl *(Athene cunicularia)*

A man walking his dog reads a recently posted sign by a large corner lot announcing a proposed development in the field where a colony of burrowing owls live. The sign proclaims the so-called advantages of the upcoming development, but what will happen to the burrowing owls? Where will they go?

I'll bet that sign doesn't say anything about the "advantages" the new development will have for the burrowing owls, because there aren't any. Those delightful little owls live in colonies that need open-space grassland areas for their burrows where they can forage for insects, small rodents, and reptiles. Now they'll have to move farther out to the Delta levees and islands to survive. That is, assuming they don't bring in the bulldozers to plow the lot in the spring when the owls are nesting in their burrows. That would be disastrous for the owls. The bulldozers wouldn't notice.

Burrowing owls don't do well in the middle of town and their populations are on the decline in California. That's what happens to wild animals who live where humans like to build things.

Great horned owl (*Bubo virginianus*)

This fearsome nighttime hunter has the largest range of all North American owls. Its eerie and vibrant "Hoo hoohoo hoo" can be heard echoing over most of the country. These stocky, powerful, broad-shouldered predators will prey on an enormous variety of animals, ranging from mice to gophers, reptiles, domestic cats, ground and tree squirrels, skunks (owls and most other birds have a poor sense of smell), opossums, and even other hawks and owls.

Great horned owls are particularly adept at plucking up the young of other species of raptors as they perch on a limb waiting for their parents to return and feed them. In the 1970s, when valiant attempts were being made to try to reintroduce captive-bred peregrine falcon chicks back into the wild to help put this endangered species back on its feet, great horned owls almost ruined several individual breeding and reintroduction

CHUKK TODD

programs before they really got started by killing and eating the peregrine chicks.

One damp fall morning, I stood in my driveway in the darkness just before dawn and let the cool rain wash the sleep out of my eyes. I always like to greet and welcome the first rains of fall. As I listened to the soft hiss of the rain whispering in my ears, there was a sudden soft "hoo huhu hoohoo" from the top of the huge deodar cedar in my neighbor's front yard. It was a female great horned owl, probably the one I used to hear every morning about this same time last year.

I tried to imitate a male's "hoo hoohoo." The only response was the louder hiss of the rain as it started to fall harder. Then from far across the little canyon behind my house—"hoo hoohoo." And she immediately answered the real male owl, again and again and again.

Was it something I said?

Another black early fall dawn, years ago, I sat on a granite boulder in the Yosemite backcountry and decided to hoot back at some "hoo hoos" in the darkness.

"Hoo hoo," said I.

"Hoo hoo!" came back from the distance.

"Hoo hoo," I replied, smugly.

"HOO HOO!" replied the great horned owl from the blackness, mere inches away as its soft wing feathers suddenly brushed across my forehead.

"Yipes!" I yelled, ducking so hard my chin bounced off my knees.

To this day I'm still amazed that it was the owl's soft wing feathers that brushed my head— and not its eight needle-tipped talons. That Mother Nature is such a kidder.

Willard: My Son the Owl

In the spring of 1970 I was handed a little gray ball of fluff. It trembled and grew two enormous yellow eyes. A rubbery wing popped from each side and a tiny beak poked out below the eyes and twittered. Two legs sprouted from the bottom and the fuzz ball suddenly teetered on my opened palm. It reminded me of Willis, the Martian roundhead in Robert Heinlein's classic novel about Mars, *The Red Planet*.

Willard was a great horned owl and I was the then fledgling curator of the Lindsay Wildlife Museum. Willard had been taken from a local nest by kids and was so imprinted to humans when we got him that he was much too tame to return to the wild. He thought he was more human than owl, and right from the beginning we both accepted that I was his foster father and he was my feathery son.

Willard's twenty-five years at the museum were an education to us all. He taught countless school children what it was like to be an owl and delighted in allowing them to touch and feel the softness of his feathers. ("So I can fly quietly and sneak up on tasty gophers in the dark, silly!")

Our own relationship had its ups and downs, as it is between all parents and their children. We were affectionate friends (ever had your beard preened by a two-inch beak?) until Willard suddenly matured and grew up into an adult owl when he was five or six. I discovered to my dismay one morning that now that he was an adult male owl, Willard considered me to be another male owl and I should get out of his space—the museum—immediately. Fortunately, I had good reflexes and he destroyed only my shirt.

We eventually managed to work things out. Sort of. I stayed in my corner of the museum and he stayed in his. Except for the one time he got loose and chased me into the office and killed my poor down jacket.

Willard hooted his way into the hearts of thousands of museum visitors over the years. Twenty-five years is a century to a great horned owl, but it seems like only yesterday I was holding that warm ball of fluff against my cheek.

Willard died on December 15, 1995, quietly in his sleep as befits an ancient wise owl of his regal stature. I missed the grumpy hoots he gave whenever this other, featherless male "owl" dropped by to visit, but I knew it was going to be okay. The fields in heaven are full of tasty gophers.

Western screech owl (*Otus kennicottii*)

A screech owl looks like a nine-inch-tall miniature great horned owl, with the same kinds of ear-like tufts of feathers above each of the eyes that flare up rigidly when it gets excited. You rarely know these little birds of prey are around because they fly in the dark and roost and nest out of sight in hollow trees, but you'll sometimes spot a gray ball of fluff perched on a ledge in your garden shed or up high in the garage.

These aggressive little raptors eat insects and arthropods and will get down and wrestle (and win!) with songbirds almost as big as they are. My wife and I were once having dinner with a friend who lived on a little farm in the hills behind Danville. We were in her kitchen washing the dishes when we heard a banging noise against the back window just above the sink. We all looked up at the same time to see a screech owl standing on the sill and hanging onto the flopping body of a dying Brewer's blackbird, its neck clinched tightly by the owl's foot. As we finished cleaning the dishes, we got to watch the floor show, starring a hungry screech owl as it plucked and ate the blackbird for dinner...or maybe I should say breakfast.

One October I received a letter from a little town in the Sierra foothills about a bird that was only active at night that had fallen down a stovepipe and become trapped in a woodstove. The letter's writers finally got the bird out after three days (thankfully the stove had been cold) and discovered what they thought was a baby owl. They took the owl outside and released it and it flew up into a tree. They wanted to know how a bird could survive three days in a wood-stove without food or water.

Because there usually aren't any baby owls flying around in the fall months, the "baby" was probably actually an adult screech owl. These miniature owls are only about nine inches tall and are often mistaken for babies. Unlike most songbirds, owls and hawks have the ability (because of a slightly lower metabolism, I think) to survive several days without eating. The owl in the stove may also have filled up on mice just before it fell in, and that was apparently enough to keep it going until they were able to set it free.

I wrote them back and suggested they put a piece of screen over the stovepipe so the poor birds wouldn't keep falling in.

Another question I hear is, Will a screech owl who has moved into a backyard birdhouse frighten away the other songbirds in the yard? Screech owls will occasionally prey on songbirds, but I don't think having that little owl rent a birdhouse is going to frighten off all its new songbird neighbors. Owls hunt mostly at night, and songbirds by day, so there's only a small window of time when their paths cross. The songbirds all know that. Unfortunately for some of them, so does the little screech owl.

Eagles ....

Bald eagle *(Haliaeetus leucocephalus)*

Bald eagles act kind of like bald-headed vultures. They spend a lot of time perched in trees along rivers and lakes looking for dead fish floating in the water. In Alaska, when thousands of salmon are rushing up the rivers to their spawning grounds, the waterway is lined with these great beautiful birds as they jostle each other and push and connive and harangue in an attempt to be the first to grab a dead or dying fish. Whereas the golden eagle primarily survives by hunting and killing prey, with an occasional stop-off to feed on fresh roadkill, bald eagles seem to prefer to con their meals from others and will usually only resort to hunting and killing their prey when they have no other choice. Unless, of course, a rabbit runs across the road in front of them. You can't let a free and easy meal go to waste, you know.

Who's In Charge Here?

Back in the 1970s when I was curator at the Lindsay Wildlife Museum I had a huge (20' x 40' foot) aviary at my home that I used as a recovery ward for injured hawks and eagles from the museum's wildlife rescue program. One evening as I sat down to dinner, a knock came at the door. It was a game warden who had brought a bald eagle with an injured (bruised) wing.

I wanted to get the bald out of the box he was being held in before he

thrashed around and hurt himself further, but I was concerned about putting him in my aviary with the six golden eagles that were living there. Golden eagles are the ultimate predators, with huge, powerful feet, piercing eyes, and a fierce inclination to kill things. Bald eagles, on the other hand, have tiny feet, sometimes cluck like chickens, and have an overwhelming interest in fish that float on top of the water. I figured if I tossed the bald into my aviary, six sets of golden talons would nail him before he hit the ground.

But then he started to bang around in the box so I decided to give it a try. We picked up the heavy box and carried it to the aviary. After a moment, out hopped the bald. He shook his white head and then the rest of his body to straighten his mussed-up feathers. Then he saw me and quickly hopped across the sandy floor of the aviary to get as far away from me as he could. His right wing drooped slightly, indicating the injury that kept him from flying.

The golden eagles couldn't have been more uninterested. I tossed each of the eagles a dead rabbit or squirrel from my refrigerator (wardens kept me supplied with roadkill) and watched as they ripped into the carcasses and started to eat. It reminded me that I was hungry, so I went back into the house to have dinner.

I'd just finished my salad when I heard a lot of horrific screaming coming from the aviary. Oh God...You won't believe what I saw when I charged into that enclosure.

In the middle of the aviary, on top of a pile of seven dead rabbits and squirrels, stood the triumphant bald eagle. His big beak was wide open as he vented victory scream after victory scream:

"My food! My food!" The six golden eagles stood in a circle around the bald, squawking in dismay, confused looks on their beaks. They knew how to soar and hunt and kill, but they hadn't a clue on how to deal with a pushy bald eagle who had stolen their food. From that day on until I transferred the bald to another facility, I had to stand in the aviary with a kitchen broom at feeding time and bop the bald eagle on his pure white head to keep him from swiping the other birds' food.

Bald eagles are relentless survivors, often under overwhelming circumstances, and they never quit. I think they make kind of a cool national emblem. Think about it.

Golden eagle (*Aquila chrysaetos*)

There are a lot of golden eagles hunting rabbits, domestic and feral cats, and squirrels and constructing their enormous platform nests in oak trees along the grassy slopes and valleys of the Mount Diablo Range. One large female eagle occasionally suns her six-foot wings atop a metal transmission tower near downtown Walnut Creek. When she's done she will sometimes tip forward off her perch, spread her wings, and go for a long, low glide over the middle of the downtown area. No one ever looks up and sees her. I've often watched that huge bird take that flight and wondered what she thought of the strange place that had replaced her beautiful fields.

Life Is Never Simple. Neither Is Killing.

I remember once, while working at a wildlife rescue center, helping to raise an orphaned golden eagle. We presumptuous humans were trying to

teach that little ball of fluff the skills it needed so it could hunt and survive on its own when we released it. Silly us for thinking we could enhance the natural instincts that were already lurking deep within its breast.

The eagle grew into a three-foot-tall predator with giant feet, enormous two-inch talons, and a great hooked beak. And one morning just after dawn, we were overjoyed when that huge bird glided down out of the sky on seven-foot wings and killed a big fat jackrabbit for its breakfast.

Then, later that same day, I spent two hours picking gravel out of the back end of another jackrabbit that had been hit by a car. The injuries were minor and the jackrabbit was released in a field near where it was found.

I've thought a lot over the years about the incongruity of my actions on that day: taking delight in helping to kill one jackrabbit and feeling an equal delight in saving and releasing another. Even now,

years later, I find it difficult to resolve the conflicting tumble of emotions that result from trying to reconcile—and justify—the two events.

So I don't try. Sometimes we're forced to oversimplify things just to understand what's going on.

Hot Stuff

Ching, a four-month-old orphan golden eagle I was rehabilitating for the Lindsay Wildlife Museum, sat on a perch in my backyard one icy winter morning in 1971. Her shoulders were encased in a layer of white frost. I chirped a "good morning" to her and pressed my finger down through the frozen crust, shoving it deep past her cold outer feathers into the hot down next to her skin.

The insulation created from the multiple layers of overlapping feathers was perfect. It was so cold I thought my foggy breath would freeze, but under her feathers that great predatory bird was *hot*. Maybe that's where golden eagles get their fiery natures.

She jumped off her perch, broke through the ice on top of the water dish with the tip of her broadsword beak and stepped demurely into the frigid waters to take her morning bath. Then, after the sun came up and dried the great bird off, I sat cross-legged on the ground in front of her and let her bend down from her perch and preen my beard with the tip of her beak. It was awesome!

Falcons...................................

American kestrel *(Falco sparverius)*

This very common little sharp-winged falcon sits on power lines and fences with its long tail bobbing up and down. It typically hunts its prey from the tops of telephone poles and fence posts, cocking its head as it looks down with sharp eyes until it spots something. A kestrel will also hover over one spot on rapidly beating wings like a tiny helicopter and drop straight down to the ground to snatch up its prey. Kestrels mainly dine on insects and small rodents, but they have also been known to grab a small bird, snake, frog, or even a big fat worm with a triumphant "klee-klee-klee!"

I once got a call from a lady who saw a "sparrow hawk" perched on her back fence. She was concerned for her three-pound poodle. She said the little raptor had been "eyeing" her dog when she and her pet were out working in the garden. Was the dog going to become hawk food? How could she protect it?

A kestrel, or sparrow hawk, is actually a little falcon that stands about nine inches tall and spends its days hunting insects, mice, and small reptiles. Dogs, even a tiny three-pound poodle, are *way* out of this little raptor's league. Kestrels are very alert and curious, so it was probably just checking out the dog and thinking, "Wow, that's a very BIG dog."

However, if that bird wasn't a kestrel and was in fact one of the larger hawks—like a red-tailed hawk (nineteen-inches tall) or a Cooper's hawk (sixteen-inches tall)—then that rabbit-size poodle might be very much at risk. The same thing goes with the great horned owls that hunt in our suburban yards after dark. A dog that small might catch their interest.

Actually, I suspect that little pooch was more at risk of getting pounded on by the neighborhood cats, which are way bigger than the dog. The cats probably drew straws to see who got first crack at the tiny poodle. I don't think I would let a dog that small go outside unless I was going to be with it at all times—especially at night.

Another of my readers was driving along and saw a stretch of power line with two pigeons on it. Standing right next to them was a kestrel. He wanted to know if the kestrel was confused, looking for friends in all the wrong places, or what? He said he'd never seen predator and prey standing side by side with each other before.

I have to agree that sometimes our crowded suburban skies can produce some strange bedfellows. Those two bird species—pigeon and kestrel—really have nothing in common. Overweight domestic pigeons are about four

inches taller and weigh almost twice as much as those sleek little falcons. Kestrels usually ignore pigeons and other birds bigger than they are. That's why my reader probably saw the birds standing together on top of that pole: "Pigeons? What pigeons?"

You'll note I said kestrels "usually" ignore other birds. If a kestrel were *really* hungry, however, I sure wouldn't want to be a big, fat, juicy couch potato pigeon standing right next to it.

Hawks ....

Cooper's hawk (*Accipiter cooperii*)

This hawk is the king-size version of the sharp-shinned hawk and it likes to harvest songbirds at your feeders, especially the fat mourning doves which it favors. Cooper's hawks are powerful fliers and will crash through dense vegetation without a thought when they are after a fleeing bird. Rodents may even be pursued on foot into the middle of your rosebushes.

I once spent the day hunting ground squirrels with a falconer who was using a trained Cooper's hawk. When the falconer would spot a ground squirrel sitting on the mound of dirt in front of its hole, he'd launch the hawk from his glove. The Cooper's would pump frantically with its short, powerful wings in a shallow dive at the ground squirrel. If the squirrel didn't see the hawk, it was over in a minute: crash, grab, bite, kill. If the squirrel saw the hawk, it was a race to see if the squirrel could reach its hole before the hawk could catch it.

On one occasion, the squirrel beat the hawk to the hole and escaped with a quick flip of its short tail in the hawk's face. The hawk was so enraged it tried to follow the ground squirrel down its hole. When we came running up, all we could see was the hawk's tail feathers wagging back and forth in the hole. It took the falconer five minutes to extract the hawk and when he did the hawk was so furious that it flew straight up at the man's head and tried to grab his face in its talons. Now *that* is a bird of prey!

Sharp-shinned hawk (*Accipiter striatus*)

You can see its long, skinny legs (sharp-shinned, remember?) when it is perched on your back fence, checking out all the plump sparrows and house finches at your feeder. These *very* aggressive hunters also like to visit your backyard feeders along with the other birds, but they are there to eat those very same songbirds, not the seeds.

Most of the sharp-shinned hawk's prey is taken by ambush. When your prey is almost as big as you are, you have to be clever. Songbirds are always keeping an eye out for "sharpies" for that very reason. If your busy feeder is suddenly deserted, the birds have probably seen one of these predators and are hiding. These little hawks also prey on rodents, bats, frogs, and insects. They get so excited sometimes I've even seen them dive down and catch leaves blowing in the wind. Look first and ask questions later, right?

Coops and Sharpies

These two bird-eating hawk species take the term "bird feeder" literally. Both have similar attitudes:

they are aggressive, athletic, focused, and deadly hunters that will hide in a nearby tree until your feeder is crowded with small birds, then swoop down and grab the biggest and fattest bird in sight during the resulting confusion.

I was once out in a field watching a ground squirrel digging a hole. I didn't know a Cooper's hawk was in the oak tree behind me until it took off in a shallow dive, lightly brushing my head as it passed, and caught the squirrel. The hawk never knew I was there. The best predators have perfect focus.

One time, my ruddy-brown Abyssinian cat, Tut, was sitting on the windowsill looking outside at one of our bird feeders when a Cooper's hawk saw him and thought he was a squirrel. There was an incredible crash between bird and window, followed by a thud as the imprint of a terrified Abyssinian cat suddenly appeared on a nearby wall.

Predatory Intelligence

Years ago, a friend of mine was a ranger at a California state park. He used to go out on the porch of his ranger house at dawn to feed a large covey of California quail while he had his morning coffee. One day, a big female Cooper's hawk joined him for her own morning treat. She came gliding in about ten feet above the ground with the rising sun at her back and her shadow preceding her on the ground by about twenty feet. When her dark silhouette passed over the feeding quail, the whole flock automatically took off—right into the flight path of the clever, hungry hawk.

My friend said the airborne hawk lazily rolled over on her side, reached out with a massive long-toed foot tipped with sharp, pointed talons, and plucked a fat quail from the sky to have for her breakfast.

Jays and mockingbirds assume the roles of town criers whenever a predator, even a small one like a screech owl, is discovered in their territories. In seconds, every bird within hearing range arrives to harass the intruder with a noisy hue and cry. (Forget Hitchcock, it's more like when the villagers discover Frankenstein's monster, as played by Boris Karloff.)

But there are exceptions. These alarmists usually don't mess with the more dangerous bird-eating raptors like Cooper's hawks. Why spoil all the fun by getting killed and eaten?

Birds have an "out of sight, out of mind" kind of mentality. I once saw a Cooper's hawk take advantage of that. The songbirds disappeared as usual when they saw the hawk in the sky, but then the predator flew around a corner, landed on the ground, and ran back to the cover of some low bushes. When the birds came out to play, the clever hawk joined them for dinner.

Red-shouldered hawk *(Buteo lineatus)*

Twenty years ago you wouldn't see many of these hawks in populated suburban and urban areas of the East Bay. But as the farmlands have given way to development, these colorful and very aggressive raptors, a little thinner and shorter than red-tailed hawks, found themselves moving closer and closer to town, whether they liked it or not. They are often mistaken for red-tails, until you get close

enough to see their longer, nar-
rower wings and tail and the
cinnamon breast feathers,
red shoulders, and broad-
banded tail feathers.

Red-tailed hawk
(*Buteo jamaicensis*)

When you are out work-
ing in your garden and
look up to see a large bird
of prey circling high above
you, it is usually a red-tailed
hawk. If the sun is positioned
just right, you can see it high-
light the rusty-red color of the tail
feathers of the adult birds. (The young
red-tails will get their adult red tail feathers in their second year. Until then, their tails
have horizontal barring kind of like a Cooper's
hawk.)

Red-tails will build large platform nests with
sticks high in trees in open space areas, but will
also occasionally use a tall oak tree in somebody's
backyard. These powerful hawks will hunt rabbits, domestic cats, squirrels, birds, snakes,
lizards, and even fish.

I heard from one homeowner who was getting
a big kick out of watching a family of red-tails living in a tree behind his house. That year there
were two chicks. It's a lot of fun watching teenage
red-tails learn how to be top-of-the-food-chain
predators. They start out all fumble and bumble
and just plain clumsy as they exercise with those
big rubbery wings. It's amazing they ever survive
to become
such skilled pilots and
fearsome hunters.

This reader's young hawks were at the stage
where they were sitting in trees around the yard
crying for breakfast, and he noticed that after the
food was delivered by the parent bird, a lot of it
fell to the ground and the young birds never went
down to recover it.

A lot of "breakfast" gets dropped by the
youngsters as they figure out what to do with
those overgrown feet. The parents stay out of it.
How else would the youngsters learn to care for
their food?

The man also noticed he had only seen one adult bird at the nest at a time, and he wondered if it took both parents to raise the chicks or if this was a single-parent family. The answer is that both parents are needed to catch enough prey for those always ravenous babies. You can tell the difference between mom and dad by their size. The female is the larger of the two. Some avian scientists think it's an advantage for a predatory bird species to have one large parent and one small one because it supposedly allows them to catch a wider range of prey species. While the female can handle the bigger rabbits, feral cats, and ground squirrels, the smaller, more maneuverable male can catch the smaller, faster animals.

One final puzzling observation of this man's red-tail family was the existence of a fox squirrel that could sometimes be seen in the same tree as the chicks but which neither parents nor babies seemed to look at or try to catch. This situation reminded me of one spring when I was observing a golden eagle nest through my binoculars. The two babies—tiny bits of white fuzz—were only a day old. A male eagle suddenly swooped down into the nest and opened one huge foot to show the bright yellow body of a tiny male American goldfinch. It was just the right size, with toothpick bones, for feeding day-old eagle chicks.

As the days went by and the babies rapidly grew, so did the size of the prey animals the parents brought to the nest for them to eat. This may be related to the man's comment about the squirrel and the seeming neutrality of the nesting tree. I once saw a huge tree with a big red-tail nest perched on the very top, several robin and finch nests here and there in the branches, a couple of barn owl nests, a great horned owl nest about four feet farther down the trunk—and a gray squirrel nest just below the owl nests. They all appeared to be living in harmony.

Getting High on Sky

Sometime every spring I like to drive halfway up Mount Diablo and watch the red-tailed hawks perform their spectacular aerial courtship maneuvers. I like to lie back in the soft, sweet-smelling grass and watch them dancing wildly across the sky, diving, pirouetting wingtip to wingtip as they swoop and wheel around each other in great concentric circles. At last, when they briefly cling together and tumble down madly through the air, if you listen closely you can hear them screaming at each other in a strange sort of angry delight. And after they disappear over a far ridge, you can sit back up and look out across the valley and pretend you can't see all the houses and freeways. You can wonder if this was the way it was a thousand years ago, before we came and messed it all up.

Vultures ....

Turkey vulture (*Cathartes aura*)

Turkey vultures—carrion eaters—soar gracefully above suburban highways and open spaces and sometimes swoop low over the housetops looking for dead things to eat. But how would you like to have turkey vulture love going on in your backyard?

That's exactly what one reader said was happening at her house, where vultures were hanging out all over her back deck, about thirty feet from the window where she was watching. She said she couldn't tell the males from the females, although she assumed that when they mated the female was the one underneath. (Correct!)

Wow, an orgy of turkey vultures on your back deck. I'm jealous!

Turkey vultures usually breed and nest in and around caves that can usually be found in local rocky cliffs. You know you have urban vultures when they prefer redwood decks to sandstone cliffs and dare to even think about nesting in your shrubbery.

But if you think pigeon poop is bad on statues and railings, you ought to experience turkey vulture poop on the deck. About twenty years ago, there was a row of eucalyptus trees that ran through the backyards of some houses in Concord. Everything on those yards—lawns, gardens, patios, mowers—was covered in a thick, white, smelly layer of you-know-what. Needless to say, the trees are no longer there.

Because the vultures survive on rotting meat, they rely on natural processes to kill off bacteria, and when they defecate, the alkaline feces coats their legs and feet in a spray that offers some protection from stray germs. This whitewash is great for sterilizing vulture feet but a little rugged when applied to back decks and the shake roofs of houses.

Turkey vultures also have other built-in cleaning mechanisms. At the end of one of the roads I used to take on my way to work every morning, there were several beautiful oak trees and, at about 7:30 a.m., a turkey vulture was just about always perched at the very top of one of those oaks with its wings completely extended. One day I stopped and watched and it stayed perfectly still, like a cross made out of a big black bird, for more than ten minutes. The vulture looked like it was sunbathing. That's because when the first light of the morning sun touches a vulture, its wings automatically pop out so the ultraviolet rays can zap any bacteria it might have picked up while eating roadkill for dinner the night before.

Even their signature naked red heads have a purpose: turkey vultures are bald so they don't get their feathers dirty when they stick their heads down deep into rotting carcasses of large animals. Now, if Mother Nature could just figure out something to do about that smell...

Mammals

Wild mammals that once inhabited open spaces where we now build our houses have learned how to survive in this unnatural suburban and urban wilderness. At night, after humans turn out the lights and jump into bed, the streets, yards, and skies come alive with the patter of little feet and the silent flapping of leathery wings.

Pallid bat *(Antrozous pallidus)*; **Brazilian free-tailed bat** *(Tadarida brasiliensis)*; **hoary bat** *(Lasiurus cinereus)*; **big brown bat** *(Eptesicus fuscus)*; **California bat** *(Myotis californicus)*

Yes, we do have bats living around us in the Bay Area and in most other communities around the country, especially if our homes are near ponds, lakes, or creeks. We usually don't notice them because they fly high above us in the dark and we humans rarely look up. (It's amazing what we don't see, day or night, because we don't do that.)

The pallid bat is one of the few bat species to land on the ground and scurry around foraging for prey. It eats a wide variety of insects, spiders, beetles, moths, and a lot of Jerusalem crickets, also known as potato bugs (at least in California). I know that last bit will make a lot of people happy. One lady wrote to tell me how she put all four legs of her bed in buckets of water to keep the potato bugs from crawling up and getting her while she was sleeping.

How to Be a Good Bat Neighbor

Put up a bat house in your backyard. But keep in mind that they won't work just anywhere. Here are a few basic rules about building a successful bat house:

- Bats drink a lot of water, so bat houses within a quarter of a mile from streams, rivers, or ponds have a better chance of attracting bats than those with no nearby water sources. Swimming pools also make excellent bat watering holes. Bats drink by swooping down and grabbing a mouthful of water on the wing.
- Don't hang your bat house in a tree like a birdhouse; fasten it to the trunk so it won't swing around. Bats like their houses high above the ground, mounted on the side of your own house up under the eaves or on a pole. Ten feet or higher is best.
- Temperature is the most important single factor in bat house living. Houses that receive more than four hours of direct sun each day seem to get the most activity. If your bat house isn't going batty, it's probably not getting enough sun. Move it to a warmer spot and see if that doesn't help. You might also want to paint the house black so it will absorb more heat. If you order a catalog from Bat Conservation International, you will find a map of the United States highlighted to show what color a bat house should be in your area.

Hotter climates should obviously have lighter-colored houses to keep them from getting too hot.

- People who live in the country seem to attract more bats than city residents. This probably has to do with the massive use of pesticides in suburban and urban yards. We're doing our infernal best to kill all the insects in our yards (and in the world!), but what we forget is that whether they are "good" bugs or "bad," they are an integral link in the endless food chain that nourishes the other creatures that live on Earth.

  Would you believe that more toxic chemicals are dumped in our yards every year than in all the commercial agriculture areas in the state? It's true. Next time you visit your local hardware or garden store to buy something, take a stroll down the pesticide aisle and take a big whiff. Then go read a few labels and see what you've been breathing. Pay particular attention to where it says "warning." It kind of makes you want to wear a big white plastic suit and a respirator when you go out to smell the flowers in your garden, doesn't it?

  The lack of all those flying insects has a definite negative effect on a flying mammal that needs to eat its own weight in insects every night. Bat species all around the world are in trouble because of this indiscriminate pesticide use.

- Be patient. It can take months to attract these tiny flying mammals.
- For more on bats, contact Bat Conservation International at P.O. Box 162603, Austin, TX 78716 (800-538-2287; www.batcon.org).

Beaver *(Castor canadensis)*

Beavers have been known to pop up in the strangest places. Once upon a time I got a call from a Walnut Creek resident who lived in a heavily wooded residential area about a block from the middle of town. A wild (that means it was still natural and hadn't been turned into a cement ditch) stretch of the old creek meandered past at the rear of his property. Something was chopping down the trees in his backyard. He thought it was beavers.

The guy said he heard a loud crash one night while watching TV, and when he turned on his patio lights and went out to see what was going on, he found a large ten-foot tree had fallen, just missing his patio roof. The foot-tall stump came to a classic point with teeth marks all around it.

Tracks led from the tree through the mud and disappeared into the dark, muddy waters of the creek. The Creature from the Black Lagoon, right? But beavers? In the middle of downtown Walnut Creek? That's impossible, I said.

So I went over and looked at the four or five felled trees that were flattening his flower beds, their stumps beautifully gnawed to perfect points, just like in all those Walt Disney movies we saw when we were kids.

It was a beaver, all right. Its trip to the middle of town was probably pretty simple. Just swim west down the Sacramento River about ten miles from Little Frank's Tract in the Delta, turn left at Pacheco Creek just before the Benicia Bridge, and paddle along south, dodging all the rusty shopping carts in the mud until you find a nice stretch of creek with lots of trees and bushes along both banks.

The beaver was eventually live-trapped and relocated back to the delta where it could do its thing without destroying someone's house.

Bobcat *(Felis rufus)*

Once I saw a picture of a bobcat and a jackrabbit huddled together under a bush on a little island in the middle of a river as a huge forest fire raged around them. Predator and prey pressed tightly against each other, seeking refuge in the only place they had left: each other. For a time, any thoughts of natural enemies were forgotten as they focused only on survival. That's an unusual side of a bobcat, which will normally kill a jackrabbit in an instant.

These wily predators will occasionally visit a yard on the farthest edge of town to grab a domestic cat or a pet rabbit that is allowed to live and hop around in a fenced-in backyard. Fences may make good neighbors but that won't stop the mighty leap of a bobcat.

Cougar (mountain lion) *(Felis concolor)*

I know from past experience that it's easy for a large domestic cat to dupe you into thinking you have just seen a mountain lion. You can especially get fooled about the cat's size if you're looking through binoculars. And if you've only seen lions in zoo cages or on the Discovery Channel, you have no frame of reference while peering through your field glasses, so it doesn't take much to talk yourself into thinking you are seeing a mountain lion.

I live on a hill in Benicia and I occasionally see a domestic cat pouncing and mousing on a hill across the canyon. A few days later there will usually be a report in the local paper's police calls section saying that someone saw a mountain lion on that hill at the same time I saw the cat.

There was a classic case of mistaken big-cat identity reported in Douglas City, California, in the late 1990s. An Abyssinian cat (just like my own domestic cat, Tut) was reportedly shot by a Department of Fish and Game warden responding to a call about a possible cougar attack. The attack turned out to be false, but not before the tawny-colored mountain lion look-alike pet cat was shot. Abbys do look like tiny ten-pound mountain lions, but they are definitely not the real thing, as the embarrassed warden soon discovered. As the cat's owner said, "If the professionals can't tell the difference between a ten-pound cat and a full-grown mountain lion, we're all in trouble."

I don't think we're in trouble. This just underscores the fact that you can easily be fooled—especially if you're excited—into thinking an animal is something it's not.

I Like My Scar

I was brushing my teeth one morning when I noticed the thin ridge of the scar on my upper lip. I hadn't paid attention to that thing for years. Scars are natural tattoos. You can't take your eyes off of them at first, and then you just don't see them anymore.

I got my little lip tattoo about twenty-five years ago when my friend Mark and I were in a local park walking the cat. The fact that it took two of us should tell you I'm not talking about a domestic cat. It was a six-month-old mountain lion cub. You know how "playful" domestic kittens are? Add fifty-five pounds and one-inch claws and you have a four-legged buzz saw that can shred things. Playfully, of course.

Back then I was curator of the Lindsay Wildlife Museum. Mark Ferrari and I were working with orphan zoo cubs, trying to develop a way to rehabilitate mountain lion babies to get them back into the wild. That's why we were observing Sashi that morning, just watching her be a normal mountain lion cub. I had assumed the role of her mom, and we were trying to figure out what a cub needed to learn to survive on its own.

It was a gorgeous day. The sun was just up and everything was drenched with dew. The cat was feeling her oats, dashing about with her ears flattened in pretend anger, her long, thick tail lashing dangerously around. We were all feeling good that morning as we ran through the trees playing hide-and-seek. Mountain lions love to play stalking games and will come bursting out of nowhere to tackle you and lie across your chest, their hot, dewy bodies steaming in the frosty morning as they lick your face with a big raspy tongue.

Sashi suddenly hopped up on the side of an oak, clinging to the rough trunk like Velcro with four paws the size of dessert plates. SPRONG, she bounced off that first oak and stuck to the side of a second oak about four feet away. And SPRONG, to a third, and a fourth trunk. The athleticism of these animals is awesome. We watched in amazement as the young cat ricocheted from one tree to another like the steel ball in a pinball game.

We didn't realize Sashi was getting closer and closer to us until she landed on the tree right next to me. Before I could step back, the energized kitten playfully reached out with a monstrous couch-pillow paw and slapped me in the face. I laughed and turned to say something to Mark and saw his eyes widen just as I sensed something on my chin. I reached up and felt the warm blood spurting out of my lip. "Oh no," I muttered, wondering how much of my face was left. I could feel where one of her claws had cut through my upper lip like a pair of scissors. Mark handed me his handkerchief and I pressed it against my mouth to try to stop the bleeding.

Suddenly there was a high-pitched yowl as the cub smelled the blood and leaped from the tree, bounding over to us. She voiced a loud moaning sound I had never heard her make before, stood up on her hind legs, and pawed gently at my chest. I leaned down to reassure her and she carefully smelled my bleeding lip with an even louder moan.

"Wow, she's really distressed that she hurt you," Mark said.

The big cat walked with her body pressed against my right leg all the way back to the van. She looked up every few minutes, moaned softly, and bumped gently against me to let me know she was there and cared.

As Mark drove us to the hospital for my eight stitches, Sashi sat behind me purring loudly with her forehead pressed against my neck, her forelegs reaching over the back of my seat and her soft paws, with those deadly claws carefully sheathed away, hugging my shoulders.

I took one more look at the scar and finished brushing my teeth. I like my tattoo.

Pet domestic cat (Felis catus); feral domestic cat (Felis catus)

I got taken to task by one of my readers one day about a column I wrote about a missing cat that was probably eaten by a coyote. The column was titled "Death is not cruel, just nature's way." The reader's argument was that domesticated house pets are not part of the wild animal food chain. The reader suggested I should have devoted my column to reminding people to protect their pets by keeping them inside permanently, safe from coyotes and other predators, and to leave the wild animal food chain to the wild animals.

But just try telling a domestic house cat that is being eaten by a coyote, or a golden eagle, or a great horned owl, or a red fox, that it's not in the process of becoming part of the food chain. I don't think it's going to believe you.

If you let your household pets out to play in local open space areas where they can be eaten by wild predators, they automatically become an active part of nature's wild food chain, like it or not. If you allow your cat to hunt wild mice, rats, squirrels, lizards, treefrogs, grasshoppers, and songbirds, it's only a matter of time until something bigger comes along and hunts your cat. This has nothing to do with an animal being domesticated and dependent on us for protection or just being our friend. This has to do with being killed and eaten.

While we may quibble a little on ecological semantics, I do agree quite strongly that our domestic pets are dependent on us for their protection. Thus it is our responsibility to protect them from wild predators, cars, disease, and anything else that threatens them. We also have the same responsibility to help protect the wild creatures that our cats kill. The only way to make all that happen is to keep our cats inside.

Coyote (Canis latrans)

After decades of being trapped and hunted, this wily canine predator has learned how to live with humans. Scientists refer to coyotes as four-legged "omnivorous opportunists," and Native Americans called the coyote "the trickster"

They dig their dens near houses and feed on mice, rats, squirrels, gophers, brush rabbits, jackrabbits, reptiles, amphibians, insects, birds (when they can catch them), and the bowl of food you leave out on the patio every night for your pets. They have also acquired a taste for feral cats they catch in open spaces, as well as domestic cats and small dogs they find as they poke around our yards at night. (I wonder if it's possible for the family dog to starve to death, even though you put food out for it on the patio every night. After the coyotes, raccoons, opossums, and skunks get finished with their snacking, there's usually nothing left for your dog. Has your pooch been looking kind of skinny lately?)

If you live near an open space area, you'll hear these wily, wild canines "yip-yip-yipping" in the night. Sometimes you'll hear them yipping even if your house isn't anywhere near an open space area, and that can be kind of weird. That's because we humans aren't the only ones who jog along the sidewalks and roam the gutters, especially in the middle of the night.

Coyote Communication

Coyotes talk a lot to communicate with other coyotes and to define their territories. They may also be responding to the sound of barking dogs. And sometimes, under the hypnotic influence of the moon, I think they howl because it just makes them feel good. Howling is a very primitive action. You should try it some time.

Years ago, I raised an Arctic wolf in a research project. When he was a year old, I took Amorak to live as the alpha wolf at the San Francisco Zoo's open air Wolf Woods enclosure. I used to go visit him early on Sunday mornings before the zoo opened, when those huge wild canids were just silent ghostly shadows in the fog.

One Sunday, as I stood on the overlook staring down into the grotto at Amorak, he raised his muzzle and let out a long, penetrating howl. Without thinking, I tipped my head and joined him, and we were both soon enveloped in a sea of howls as the other members of his pack joined in. Never before or since have I been filled with such an overwhelming sense of primitive animal emotion. A human and a wolf pack, squeezed together in the hands of the fog, linked forever by our howling, and for a brief incredible instant we were one. It was a very interesting, very special moment. Wanna see my fangs?

How to Be a Good Coyote Neighbor

Number one: Don't feed the coyotes. Number two: Make your cats real house pets and keep them inside. My cats, Tut-the-Butt and Hello Newman, are indoor cats and they will live up to five years longer than domestic cats that are allowed to go outside. Outside cats get more diseases than indoor cats. They also run the risk of being run over by cars, chased and killed by dogs, captured and eaten by wild predators, and harassed and injured by unthinking humans. If you can't deal with making your cats permanent inside cats, for sure keep them in at night. Your cats' lives will depend on it and you'll help keep those coyotes from getting into trouble.

Black-tailed deer (*Odocoileus hemionus*)

Deer feed in East Bay gardens and roam up and down the streets and sidewalks at night. It's always kind of a shock to go out and check your garden in the morning before work and find the ground full of hoof prints and your prize-winning roses munched down a few canes.

Deer wander the streets at night and blend into foliage so well they can sleep all day under your ceanothus and you never even notice them. In the spring, the odorless spotted fawns are left by the doe to nap invisibly and well-camouflaged in yards while she goes off foraging. If you find a fawn, back off and let it be. It is not lost.

Several years ago, a UC Berkeley professor started a study on urban deer. He reported that some deer spend their entire lives in the city—born in somebody's backyard and eventually killed on city streets. As local open spaces dwindle and disappear, deer are drawn into closer contact with humans. They are too big to hide under a house and they are vulnerable to cars and people who don't want them eating their gardens. Local officials are always looking for ways to manage deer problems. And that's always bad news for the deer.

Gray fox (*Urocyon cinereoargenteus*)

This shy little fox is nocturnal and feeds on rodents, birds, berries, and insects. It is rarely seen in urban areas and has probably retreated from close human contact and from its pushy red fox cousins that seem to thrive around people.

In 1985, something was eating grapes from a backyard vine near downtown Walnut Creek. A gray fox was found living in a hollow in a nearby oak tree. It slept all day and came out at night to forage in neighboring yards. The fox disappeared shortly after its hollow hideaway was discovered.

How to Be a Good Deer Neighbor

Don't feed the deer. If deer get used to being fed by you, they will expect the same treatment from your neighbors. Since that's not always the case, it tends to create some, ahem, rather "interesting" problems and outright feuds.

Suburban deer are too tame as it is and that, plus antlers and sharp hooves, produce a potentially dangerous animal if something frightens one in the tight confines of a yard. The regular source of food makes them hang around when they should be off in the hills, and this puts them at risk for disastrous daytime encounters with dogs, cars, and less-understanding people.

The things you might put out for a deer, say, a salt block, oats, and hay, are cattle feed, and a deer's digestive systems and tastes are more inclined to deal with roughage than hay. Deer browse on leaves, new shoots, green twigs, bark, acorns, your roses, apples, etc. If there are deer hanging around, that means your yard is already providing them with what they want in a pleasant, low-key, natural way. Don't spoil things by trying to get fancy.

Of course, you may not want the deer to feed in your garden. I had a friend who had deer vaulting his six-foot redwood fence and gobbling his roses. He added to the height of his fence by running an eighteen-inch extension of chicken wire around the top of the fence. He left it loose (no tension) and wobbly, and this rippling effect made the already hard-to-see top edge of the wire even less defined. In the twilight and dark it was tough to see it at all. The attacks on his roses stopped and everyone lived happily ever after. The deer moved on and foraged and found things to eat in a nearby open space area where they really belonged.

Wobbly top and eight-foot fences are the only obstacles that really "repel" deer. (They also have another "bonus benefit," as my friend called it: neighborhood cats can't find a way over them either.) Repellents (commercial ones like Ropel, along with Irish Spring soap and other homemade powders and bad smells) usually work until the deer get really hungry. The same with lining your yard with unappetizing plants: deer won't eat them until there's nothing else to eat.

But if food is plentiful, you can usually keep deer away by using deer repellents and landscaping with not-so-tasty plants. Most nurseries have a selection of woody plants that deer don't like. Repellents work by teaching deer to stay away from your garden, and you should start using them in the fall before springtime browsing begins.

Suburban deer get chased a lot by dogs. I'm sure they feel threatened, frightened, maybe angry, or even all of the above; they have no way of knowing what's going to happen if a dog catches them. In most cases, neither does the dog. Unfortunately, the thrill of the chase to meet new playmates is often followed by the thrill of the kill, and even the gentlest of family dogs can lose control and fall prey to its own primal hunting instincts.

A game warden told me a story about trying to track down a pack of dogs that was chasing and running deer into San Pablo Reservoir several mornings a week and then running up and down the banks as the frantic deer swam around in a circle until they drowned. The warden picked a spot behind a big boulder on a little hill above the reservoir and trained the telescopic sight on his rifle on the deer trail below him. He could hear yapping and barking in the distance and soon three deer came bounding up the trail. Close behind, he could hear the pack of dogs. The warden bent over and shoved the stock of the rifle tightly against his shoulder and peered through the sight, waiting for the first dog to come running down the trail. And what to his wondering eyes should appear but...a Daschund, a miniature poodle, a Chihuahua, and a fox terrier, all hot on the trail of the fleeing deer.

"I took my finger off the trigger just in time," he laughed. And then he followed the little dogs back to their homes and wrote out tickets to each of the dogs' humans.

Would a deer attack a dog that chases it? It's happened. A deer could just as easily be severely injured or kill itself by fleeing into a barbed wire fence. That's happened, too.

It's best to carry a leash when walking your dog in open spaces, and be prepared to quickly snap it on your pet's collar when you encounter deer or any other wildlife. That way, no one gets hurt— the animal, your dog, and sometimes even you.

Eastern red fox *(Vulpes vulpes regalis)*

Before California made it illegal to purchase and keep Eastern red foxes as pets in the early 1970s, many escaped (or were released) and a large population eventually became established in the San Francisco Bay Area. They are larger and more gregarious (with humans) than the shy, short-legged native gray foxes, often raising their cubs under the back decks of suburban homes. They also will prey on the cats that live in those suburban homes. Clever red foxes.

The Red Coats (Foxes) Are Coming

Twenty years ago, you rarely saw a fox, never a coyote, occasionally a deer dead on the road, and you marveled at the rare raccoon on your fence, stopped to get a good look at the opossum squinting in your headlights, and always ran around closing all the windows when you smelled a skunk.

Today, I regularly hear of red foxes denning under back decks in suburban East Bay communities. One homeowner reported he was barbecuing chicken one Sunday and turned around to find a family of foxes lined up drooling and awaiting their turn.

Broad-footed mole
(*Scapanus latimanus*)

Moles are not gophers, although they both leave mounds of dirt in your yard. If there's no hole in the ground next to the dirt pile, it was probably made by a mole. These are the little gray-coated critters that sometimes leave the zig-zag tunnels half-submerged in your lawn.

These burrowing mammals are not rodents (like the gopher). They are insectivores, using their needle-sharp teeth to crunch insects, earthworms, spiders, centipedes, and even small mammals. They could care less about munching on your plants...well, except for an occasional out-of-control foray into your iris rhizomes (which harbor iris borers).

Got a mole that's making its mark on your finely manicured lawn and driving you crazy? You've got the wrong attitude. Think positive.

If you didn't have moles to churn up the soil under your yard, you'd have to hire a gardener to come aerate your lawn. If you didn't have moles to gobble up all those lawn beetle larvae that are eating your grass and leaving *their* mark, you'd have a troop of raccoons peeling back your lawn and carting it off to sell at the flea market. That's right: moles are our friends, although the greenskeepers at your local golf course might take issue with this.

See? There's always a silver furrow in your lawn if you take the time to look for it. (It's right behind the mole.)

If the Mole Just Can't Stay

If you absolutely cannot tolerate having that friendly little mole sticking around in your yard to help you aerate your lawn, here's how to humanely capture your moles and relocate them to a friendlier environment.

When I was just a kid, a wise old owl stopped by just outside my bedroom window one night and told me how to catch a mole. Maybe it was an owl and maybe it was just a dream. I watched a lot of television in those days. Here's what it told me:

If you find a fresh mole tunnel, carefully excavate a one-foot stretch of the tunnel, taking care not to collapse the rest. Then dig a hole in the middle of the tunnel, as big around as and deep enough to hold an empty five-pound coffee can. Push the can down into the hole so that it sits just below the surface of the tunnel floor, creating a metal-lined pit.

Then remove all signs of your visit and place a piece of cardboard over the excavated area (put a roof back over the tunnel) and cover it lightly with earth to block out all light. This will allow

How to Be a Good Mole Neighbor

Sooner or later every spring, a mole sticks up a little periscope in the middle of my lawn, checks out the area, and then proceeds to poke around my yard—literally. We have a lot of flowers and a large garden, so I'm always more than mildly interested in what happens out there.

After several weeks of shallow, random tunneling and the occasional small mound of dirt pushed up as it searches for tasty earthworms, the mole rarely damages a single plant. The ridges of its shallow tunneling have never appeared in the lawn, only in flowerbeds and dirt areas. It's easy to remove the dirt piles, and I figure the little guy aerates miles of the hard clay soil under my yard. What a deal. When the mole disappears, as it always does, I wait for the screams from my neighbor.

you to come back every hour to check on your coffee can trap. (Moles have a high metabolism and need food every hour or so, so DO NOT be late or you can starve the poor mole to death.) According to the wise old owl, when the mole runs through its tunnel, it falls into the coffee can pit and can't climb back out with its short digging legs. If you find the mole when you come to look, put the lid on the can (careful, as these critters can bite) and quickly transport it to a nearby wooded area where it can take up landscaping without bothering anyone. Find an area where the earth is soft and there are lots of plants around and dig a hole in that soft earth about a foot deep or so and release the mole down in the hole so it can dig a new hole before it runs into any predators.

There is one thing to look out for when using this technique. You might stick your coffee can in an old abandoned tunnel. That means you'll need to find a fresher, more active tunnel to get any action. I know a guy who found nothing but old tunnels and ended up with a lawn looking worse than when he started. By that time the mole had found a mate and started a family under his roses. This is where I remind you that nobody's perfect. Not even wise old owls.

Muskrat (*Ondatra zibethicus*)

One reader saw an animal the size of a small cat gathering grass and leaves along the waterline from the bank of a creek just behind his house. It swam away with a mouthful of greenery, finally disappearing under the water. It was sleek, gray-brown with a black tail, and it was a really good swimmer. He wanted to know what the creature was.

It sounded like a muskrat to me. These aquatic rodents are pretty common in local waterways. I've seen them cruising down several of the cement-lined "creeks" that meander through the downtown area of Walnut Creek, and they're pretty common in most of the community ponds in the area. During one heavy winter rainstorm several years ago, a muskrat was spotted swimming upstream in a flooded gutter in Pleasant Hill. That suburban muskrat probably thought the gutter was a creek. Actually, it was, as far as the muskrat was concerned. Muskrats have webbed hind feet and mostly feed on water plants—they really like cattails! The one my reader saw probably lives in a den it burrowed in the side of the creek bank with an underwater entrance.

Virginia opossum (*Didelphis virginiana*)

These marsupials (yes, the animals with the furry little pocket on the female's stomach) are so plentiful in some suburban and urban areas that one out of every three human residents probably has one using their yard. We rarely encounter them because they are nocturnal. They sleep soundly while we humans are awake and they wake up to prowl the neighborhood when we are asleep. Many opossums are killed by cars and dogs, but that hasn't stopped their steady urban population growth since being introduced in California sometime in the early 1900s.

I'll never forget the lady who called me to say there was a twenty-pound rat in her backyard.

"Do they eat cats?" she yelled into the phone.

"It won't eat your cat," I soothed. "And it's not a rat; it's an opossum."

"That's the biggest rat I ever saw in my whole life!" she yelled, nearly rupturing my eardrum. "Do they eat dogs?"

"No, ma'am, that opossum won't eat your dog."

"I don't have a cat or a dog and I know a rat when I see one! That's the biggest rat I ever saw in my life! You're no help!" she yelled, hanging up.

That's the way it is with animal writers and opossums. We're always getting a bad rap.

I've always been fascinated by opossums. To me, these chubby marsupials are the very essence of instinctive behavior. How else could one of the dumbest animals in the animal kingdom survive?

But wait, you say. How can you call an animal with the smarts to play dead, dumb? Ah, I counter, "smarts" is in the eye of the beholder. Opossums don't play dead—they faint. Something scares them and they go into shock and keel over, which gives the dog or other predator time to stroll over and discover that the green stuff oozing from the opossum's rectal scent glands smells really bad. By the time the opossum comes to, the danger has passed and it wanders off in its never-ending search for food.

So what else has Mother Nature done to help this nocturnal animal make it through an average night? (Making it through the day is easy. It's probably snoring away in a corner of your garage or under your deck, even as we speak.) Opossums bring new meaning to the term "omnivorous." I have a theory that opossums could probably survive on a diet of dry grass, but of course they don't have to since we provide them with a scrumptious smorgasbord of leftover garbage, heaping bowls of cat and dog food on our patios, and gardens full of tasty fruits and vegetables. In between this gourmet dining, there is also plenty of natural food in the form of insects (potato bugs: yum!), small rodents, and earthworms.

Opossums are also physically equipped to handle just about any situation without thinking. They have prehensile tails, which they use to hang on while they nap in the crotch of a tree. Their feet are like little hands (recognize those muddy prints on your deck?) and can grip just about anything. Their hind feet even have opposable thumbs, which would be handy if they ever took up sign painting.

Opossums also have excellent hearing, an incredible sense of smell, and more teeth (fifty) than any other mammal in North America. They are not aggressive but are quite willing to open up their huge mouths and display all those shiny white teeth if you ask. Fortunately for them, since they aren't good fighters, this bluff usually works.

They are also immune to most of the common animal diseases. They don't get distemper and they appear to have some resistance to rabies although, like all mammals, they *can* get it.

Most important for their survival as a species, opossums make lots of babies. They are sexually mature in the first year, they breed anytime, anywhere, and they can produce two batches of four to ten babies annually. The pea-sized babies are born after twelve and a half days of gestation, after which they wiggle into mama's pouch and swallow a nipple for the next month or so. When it gets too crowded in that stuffy pouch, the youngsters climb onto mom's back and hang on for dear life as she jogs through our yards. Occasionally one bounces off, and when it hits the ground, it's on its own.

I'll let you in on a little secret. They really do look like big rats. But they aren't.

You Say You Found an Opossum in Your Garage?

Relax. There's nothing wrong with an opossum sleeping in your garage. Hundreds of opossums are probably sleeping in hundreds of garages in your town, even as we speak, and no one knows about it (uh, until now). Your opossum is a gentle creature and won't hurt you or your cat. If your cat is sleeping in your garage too, it knows about the opossum and is probably not a bit bothered. I've seen an opossum and a cat eating out of the same food dish together.

If you want the opossum out of your garage, clean up all the hiding places and it will move on. Otherwise, the opossum will sleep all day and roam at night while you roam all day and sleep at night, and never the twain need meet. There's no need for you to bother the animal control folks about this. They have lots of bigger problems to deal with.

River otter (*Lutra canadensis*)

A friend of mine lives on twenty acres directly across from the Antioch Reservoir (where new houses are going up almost every day). A lot of different kinds of wild creatures pass through his yard, including coyotes, raccoons, opossums, quail, and doves. Recently, he spotted a new one—a big river otter swimming along the shore of the reservoir. When he called me, he said he was curious as to how it got there (two miles from the river with no stream inlet, just a pipeline filling the reservoir).

Let's see...If the otter started out at sunup and swam up a finger of Dutch Slough, in Oakley, to the Contra Costa Canal, and then paddled west in the canal to where it borders Antioch Community Park, he would only have to waddle across the golf course for one quarter of a mile to the reservoir—and he'd still have time to play nine holes before he jumped in the reservoir and had those fat, tasty bluegill all to himself for dinner. Some day, Thomas Bros. Maps should put out a *Thomas Guide of Wildlife Trails*. The local wildlife would buy them up by the thousands. A striped skunk getting lost in the middle of town is a real bummer.

There once was a lone mallard drake swimming in a big pond in the middle of Walnut Creek when a river otter suddenly surfaced and grabbed its tail feathers in its jaws. The duck quickly recovered and took wing, quacking loudly, to the far side of the pond. He left the otter treading water with a mouthful of feathers. Was the otter just playing a practical joke on the unsuspecting duck or actually trying to catch it?

River otters burn up a lot of energy during a day's fun and feed on many prey species such as fish, crayfish, frogs, muskrats, marsh birds and, occasionally, ducks. They're also very playful, and grabbing a sneaky mouthful of tail feathers is a classic otter trick. It also could have been an old otter kidding around or a young otter learning how not to hunt big ducks.

Wild pig *(Sus scrofa)*

Several days after Christmas one year, some Danville residents encountered an unusual holiday surprise. Next to their back porch were "two enormous piles of a most strange-looking animal defecation." They told me the two piles were filled with what looked to be "barely digested, very large nuts or large seeds, pods or fruit that had fallen from the oak trees or other trees that fill our backwoods." They wanted to know what kind of wild animal would eat such matter and then defecate such a huge pile.

Just across the road from their house are the foothills of Mount Diablo, and immediately behind their house is a large wooded area that surrounds a beautiful creek. Their lot extends down to the creek and is not fenced in. The house gets visits from squirrels, raccoons, and wild turkeys, but the droppings left near their porch were much too big for any of those animals. They suspected a bear.

I'll narrow it down for you: those mighty poopers were wild pigs.

Bears and pigs are the only wild critters that could defecate such big seed-filled piles. And since there are no bears around here (yet!), that leaves wild pigs. I have also seen similar piles up on Mount Diablo, where those rowdy pigs have been rototilling and destroying the landscape for years. There are approximately one hundred wild pigs or more up on Diablo at the time of this writing, and it's pretty common for them to leave the mountain during the fall months when the grass and hills have dried out and come down to forage on the lush green lawns and tasty gardens around Danville and in the nearby gated community of Blackhawk.

Those green lawns in the valley are very attractive to pigs, so the Danville residents better be on the alert for a return visit next year. Pigs are like elephants; they never forget a delicious lawn.

Next time, besides more piles of you-know-what, they may also find their lawn has been plowed and abused in a rather piggish manner.

Black-tailed jackrabbit (*Lepus californicus*)

Where are all the jackrabbits? We used to be able to drive down any road and see jackrabbits, both alive and dead. The biggest problem is a loss of habitat in suburban areas. Unlike many wild creatures that can learn to adapt to living in close proximity to us humans, jackrabbits need the open fields that are now filled with shopping malls and condominiums. As the fields disappear, there are fewer and fewer jackrabbits around our suburban homes to be seen or to be run over by the cars.

Curious world, isn't it, where we get concerned when we stop seeing dead animals lying on the road?

Brush rabbit (*Sylvilagus bachmani*)

Brush rabbits are usually only seen in the yards of houses next to wild open space areas. I'm not sure if it's because they are afraid to move deeper into inhabited areas or if it's just because these tiny bunnies have little chance to make it past the many dogs and cats that prowl those yards day and night.

Raccoon (*Procyon lotor*)

Urban raccoons really have it good, with their own swimming pools, hot tubs, lawns full of yummy earthworms and tasty beetles, and free showers (sprinklers) to wash in before they head off to bed before the sun comes up.

When they're not poking around in your garbage to see if last night's dinner suits their taste or sniffing for the treefrogs in your geraniums, raccoons sleep in attics, under houses, in hollow trees, and down in the cool storm drains during the summer when it isn't raining. When they get bored, they slip in through the cat door and poke around in your kitchen cabinets to see what kind of dry breakfast foods you have. Suburban raccoons grow up to be a lot bigger than their much-wilder country cousins because they eat the same fattening foods that we humans do. I'll bet you didn't know humans were contagious, did you?

One year a lady called from Richmond to tell me that spring must be here because the previous afternoon a family of five raccoons popped out of a manhole in the middle of town and wandered off down the sidewalk looking in display windows. She went into a store to do some shopping and when she came out again, she saw the raccoons standing in line behind two street people, waiting their turn to browse through a dumpster. It's a classic symptom of spring fever in raccoons when they don't cut in line.

I think the raccoons and other wild creatures that make their homes in urban and suburban areas have been corrupted by their concrete and asphalt and plastic ecosystems. It's the land of rent-free birdhouses, overflowing bird feeders, free-swinging dog/cat/raccoon doors, endless worm-filled lawns, tasty flower beds, topless garbage cans, and free snails for everyone.

But spring fever also has a dark side. Not only are the raccoons overweight, but the deer have a taste for our American Beauty roses, and all the seed-eating birds burp black-oil sunflower seeds when they open their chubby little beaks to sing. Our birdbath is carefully placed too far from the nearest bush for a cat or a raccoon or a fox to pounce on bathing birds without giving them plenty of time to escape.

A golden-crowned sparrow had the fever once and was really enjoying himself—thrashing about in the warm spring sun and cool water as diamond droplets added sparkle to his crown.

The neighbor's gray cat, hiding in his usual spot behind the peach tree, made his usual fruitless leap. The sparrow smiled, casually shook the water from his feathers, smoothed his eyebrows, and leisurely launched himself into the air...SMACK! into the hungry talons of a diving Cooper's hawk that had been hiding in the redwood tree, just waiting for this moment.

Spring fever. It doesn't always do a body good. I wonder what the raccoon thought when it arrived that night to drink from the birdbath and found it filled with feathers. A twinge of jealousy, maybe?

White Raccoons

A friend was driving home around midnight when her headlights picked up what appeared to be a white cat in the road ahead. When it turned its head to look at the oncoming car, she realized, much to her surprise, that it was actually a raccoon.

Ah, yes, white raccoons. The ultimate adaptation for survival in gridlocked suburbia. See, it's harder to run over them when they're white. There are actually two types of white raccoons roaming around the Bay Area. The albinos have pink eyes and barely discernable yellowish face masks and tail rings. And the plain old non-albino white raccoons have dark eyes and chocolate masks and tail rings. Both types run the lack-of-color spectrum from white (rare) to yellow or blond (more common).

I wonder if anyone who has seen these occasional ghostly apparitions ever thought their house was haunted by raccoons?

Ringtail cat (*Bassariscus astutus*)

A young man once wrote me about his octogenarian parents, who he said either had a ghost or a very clever animal living somewhere in their home. When his mom went to get some candy out of a new box, she found wrappers on the floor all around, although the box itself was closed. When she picked up the box, it was empty! She blamed her husband, but he denied taking the candy.

They tried to trap the candy thief over the next few days, but the traps were always empty, with the peanut butter bait licked from the trigger, the traps never sprung. The son wanted to know what I thought it could be. He said whatever it was had certainly added a bit of excitement to their lives.

Even though mice like candy, this animal was clearly too big and aggressive for a mouse, and squirrels are day creatures and rarely raid houses. The house was in Hemet, in Riverside County in the Southern California desert, so they could

How to Be a Good Raccoon Neighbor

• Don't feed the raccoons. You will be helping to make these animals tamer than they already are. You will also be teaching them to rely on humans for food instead of learning to forage and hunt naturally.

• Deal with their lawn rolling humanely. During the fall, winter, and spring months, raccoons will prowl your front and backyards in search of earthworms, lawn beetle larvae, and other tasty critters that live in your lawn. They forage through the grass with their hand-like paws, rolling up huge strips of your lawn in the process. The effect can be quite shocking when you open the back door and look out at the remains of your lawn the next morning. One man, who had laid out rolls of fresh sod in his backyard on a Saturday, looked out Sunday morning to see that a large part of his new sod lawn had been rolled back up, seemingly waiting to be hauled off by "lawn stealers." He called the local police, who informed him that raccoons had done the dirty deed.

There are many ways to deal humanely with raccoon lawn rollers. One of the best solutions I know is the Scarecrow brand motion-activated sprinkler, which is available at many hardware and garden supply stores (or call the Scarecrow Company at 800-767-8658 for a brochure and a list of local dealers). When raccoons, deer, skunks, and your neighbor's cat are detected by the sprinkler's optic sensor, it fires a harmless but surprising blast of water at them, usually frightening them off. Then it automatically resets and waits for the next intruder.

A quick and dirty way to protect your lawn from raiding raccoons is to pick up a roll of chicken wire from the hardware store and roll it over the area of the lawn where the raccoons are digging. You can stake it down with wooden pegs. When the raccoons can't get to your lawn, they'll go bother your neighbors. The chicken wire "lawn fence" works so well, I know one homeowner who left it on his lawn permanently. When the grass grows up through the wire mesh, he mows it.

• Clean up rooftop bathrooms. Shake roofs are usually the raccoon outhouses of choice. Some of them even carve little crescents into the individual cedar shingles...Sorry, just kidding. I couldn't help myself. Nevertheless, I suspect a lot of homeowners out there in the suburban wilderness would get a big surprise if they peeked up on their roofs.

For some reason, raccoons prefer to do their flushing on rooftops. Maybe they like a bathroom with a view or the sound of water gurgling down the gutters. But jokes aside, this can actually be a serious problem. The first thing I would do to deal with it is take up a plastic bag to dispose of the feces and a hose to clean up the area. Be sure to wear rubber gloves and a gauze mask (check with your local health department to find out what kind of mask is appropriate for maximum protection) because raccoons can carry a type of roundworm that can be passed along to humans.

Remove and wash your clothes immediately after you finish cleaning the area.

Once the roof has been washed, I'd spray some clean rags with dog repellent and leave them lying around the problem area. Raccoons have sensitive noses and really hate that stuff. Rain washes off the repellent, but that should also send the raccoons scurrying off to find a dry spot to powder their noses, giving you a chance to spray new rags for after the storm.

- Share your trees. Raccoons have many different sleeping spots, and one of the most unusual is in the top of palms and other trees. But why do they climb them instead of finding a cozy spot closer to the ground? We need to put ourselves in the places of the animals on this one. What we humans see is a palm tree. What the raccoons (and fox squirrels, pigeons, barn owls, great horned owls, blackbirds, starlings, sparrows, house finches, swallows, and assorted bats) see is the ultimate condominium complex. Palm trees have more than enough nooks and crannies for everyone up top where all those huge leaves come together. They are also easy to climb. Most of the different animal species that use them get along together, abiding by a kind of unwritten rule not to prey on their neighbors.

I've seen sparrows nesting and raising their babies in palms, two feet away from little falcons that usually catch them for food. I'm sure the raccoons and squirrels work out a similar arrangement: raccoons hunt at night while the squirrels sleep, and the squirrels are off hunting nuts while the raccoons snooze away the day.

Raccoons actually travel a regular circuit that weaves through their urban and suburban territories every night as they visit the best feeding spots. The availability of food (pet food leftovers on patios, garbage-can smorgasbords, vegetables and fruit in the garden, fishpond treats, and lizards, mice, frogs, toads, insects, and assorted other goodies found along the way) is what defines the size of the individual feeding territories. During the spring, they usually don't have to travel far to eat because food is plentiful. In the fall or during times of drought, they may have to travel farther to fill their bellies.

If you kept track of the times your local raccoons visited your yard, you'd discover they are hitting your house about every second or third night as they make their rounds. This means they don't always sleep in the same spot every day. Raccoons have lots of sleeping dens sprinkled throughout their territories so they always have a place to stay when the sun comes up.

Trees that grow in our yards are good places for a wild animal to sleep when it's not foraging for food. Most trees usually have small hollows in dead branches or areas of thick foliage where a raccoon can curl up in a fork and sleep out of sight from the ground.

One of the best ways to get along with your raccoon neighbors is to share your trees and don't give the raccoons a hard time when you catch them climbing. Better to have raccoons swinging from those branches than from the rafters of your garage.

have been getting a visit from a desert wood rat. But the son's "ghost" comment led me to think it might be another animal—a ringtail cat. This domestic-cat-size animal has huge dark eyes, big ears, and a very long, fluffy ringed tail. Ringtails are nocturnal and so fast and quiet that people rarely even know they exist. Their ability to squeeze through any hole their head fits through makes it seem as if they can pass through walls and has earned them the "ghostly" label. In addition to feeding on rodents, they also eat berries and soft fruits, so I can easily imagine one raiding a candy box.

In the early part of the last century, ringtails were welcomed in the cabins of gold miners because they cleaned out the mice and wood rats. They still do that today. I periodically get mail from a couple who live on a sailboat that's tied up at a local marina on the Sacramento River. They have a ringtail that lives on their boat and dashes down the gangplank every night to forage for meals on dry land. Kind of neat, don't you think?

This gentle little creature is usually not afraid of humans and should not be harmed. I told the son to have his parents check with their local animal control folks or humane society and see if they could borrow a humane live-trap. That way, they could catch the midnight snacker without hurting it and release it someplace farther into the desert. Nobody would get their fingers or toes pinched and nothing would get its neck broken by a rat trap.

Personally, if it was my house, and it *was* a ringtail, I'd set up a little feeding station in the kitchen and tell my friends the house was haunted!

Botta's pocket gopher (*Thomomys bottae*)

Gophers are not moles, although they both leave big mounds of dirt in your yard. If there is a hole in the ground next to the dirt pile, it was probably made by a gopher. This very active burrowing rodent is an herbivore that likes to eat roots, bulbs, and stems, often pulling the whole plant deep into its tunnels. Gophers forage above ground at night (when the darkness is supposed to make it safe for them to come out of their holes) and are caught by owls, skunks, and cats.

Gophers will have one to four litters of two to twelve baby gophers from late winter to summer and sometimes longer. The life span of a gopher is about four years, unless it lives in your backyard; then it lives forever.

Urban Gopher Myths

When talking about gophers, there is more misinformation out there in the wide, wide world than there is fact. Your mailbox is regularly filled with unsolicited catalogs extolling the virtues of page after page of fancy, expensive, "guaranteed," "long-term," "cost-effective" "solutions" to your gopher troubles. There's only one problem. Most don't work.

Anything electronic and expensive is always popular, right? From what I've discovered, electronic "sonic" machines that project assorted sound frequencies (vibrations) into the ground appear to be a joke because all the professional pest control people I've talked to laugh when I mention them. The same goes for battery-powered vibrating spikes or wind-powered "clack, clack" windmills. You probably cause the same sort of vibrations by stomping angrily around your yard every time you find a new gopher hole, but does that work?

Many "natural" gopher controls also show questionable results, especially when attempts are made to test them. The gopher purge plant *(Euphorbia lathyris)* supposedly has an odor or taste that repels gophers. For the past thirty-plus years that I've been writing about animals, I've periodically asked people who have tried this plant if it works. A few say it's great, but most say the plant, which grows to three or four feet and in all directions, is worse than the gophers.

Sticking a garden hose down a gopher hole and turning on the water is just as ineffective—at least with gophers. And it can damage your water bill. Used (smelly) cat litter, which, sigh, I used to promote when I was younger and under the mental control of a diabolical cat, also rarely works.

Adding to the mix are the suburban gopher myths that have been around since the first lawn was planted.

Myth: Pour dried instant mashed potatoes down a new gopher hole. The gopher will gobble them down and the next time it drinks water it will swell up and explode.
Fact: Ha, ha, ha, ha, ha, ha!
Myth: Sprinkle ground glass in the hole and the gopher will die after eating it.
Fact: Why would a gopher feel compelled to eat ground glass?
Myth: Gophers' stomachs will swell up and they will die after eating bubble gum.
Fact: Gophers love to blow bubbles, and the popping sounds will drive you crazy.

Roof rat *(Rattus rattus alexandrinus)*

If something is eating all the peel off your lemons while the fruits are still hanging on the tree, it is probably one of these nimble rodents. They strip fruit from trees, raid garbage cans, gobble up the food we leave outside for our pets, and nest in attics, rafters, walls, ivy, and palm tree condominiums. If you have roof rats, contact your county or city vector-control agency for advice.

How to Be a Good Gopher Neighbor

There are three basic ways to effectively deal with gophers:

- Poison them. Because we humans do this, every year dogs, cats, raccoons, opossums, and birds die when they eat that gopher poison. There is also the risk of children finding the stuff. This is definitely *not* a good idea, so don't do it. I just brought it up because I knew you were going to think about it.
- Trap them. There are some very effective traps on the market (check with your local garden nursery). They are also safe to use around pets and other wildlife. But you *do* have to kill the gopher. Some of you will find it easy to do, but others won't be able to deal with it. You need to think about it before you decide on this option.

  Another big problem with poisons and traps is that you have to keep using them every time a new gopher pokes its head up through your lawn. It is never-ending.
- My favorite environmental, nontoxic, painless, humane, and permanent solution to gophers is to prevent them before they happen. Fence them out of your yard. Dig a narrow three-foot-deep trench around the inside of your fence. If you can't go down that far, dig as deep as possible. Then place an underground chicken wire fence in the trench all around the inside perimeter of your yard and shovel the dirt back in. Use one-inch mesh so tree roots can pass through the fence.

  If that's too much for you, just put an underground fence around your garden. If you do that, be sure to have the chicken wire fencing extend *above* the ground for at least twelve inches to catch the ones that poke their heads out. Gophers come out of their holes regularly to gobble surface plants at night. That's how the barn owls catch them.

Ornate shrew (*Sorex ornatus*)

Shrews are not rodents. They are mouse-like insectivores with razor-sharp upper incisors and long skinny snouts like moles. Actually, a tiny shrew is about the size of a normal mole's snout. These three-inch-long (and smaller) mammals come equipped with a super-high metabolism and live a short, fast, and presumably happy life in the backyard jungle of your lawn or flowerbed, eating insects, earthworms, and other invertebrates. The adults burn out and die of old age by the end of their second summer.

Striped skunk (*Mephitis mephitis*)

Skunks are laid-back critters and it takes a lot (like a foolish dog) to make them haul out the heavy artillery. They prowl our yards at night (look for the tunnel under your fence), foraging for insects, rodents, snails, and fallen fruit. They often supplement their natural fare with pet food, if they get lucky. That narrow three-inch-long trench—that one over there, the chocolate-colored scar in the middle of your pristine green lawn—is where the skunk scooped out the soil with its two-inch front claws looking for an earthworm. You better hope he didn't get lucky, because then he'll be back.

Skunks are also the main vectors of rabies in California, which is the primary reason—besides the horrible smell—that it's important to keep your distance from these animals. Even a healthy-looking skunk can be harboring this fatal disease. If a particularly bothersome skunk needs to be trapped by a county trapper, it is often euthanized and delivered to the county health department to be checked for rabies. If there has been *any* human contact with the animal, it will *definitely* be taken to the department and checked for rabies. The only guaranteed way to find out for sure whether or not an animal has the disease is to kill it so a slice of tissue can be removed from its brain and stained with a special dye that will show if the rabies virus is present.

Baby skunks are particularly tempting because they are so cute, but you should resist the urge to pick them up and play with them. If the baby skunks appear to be lost or orphaned, that makes them an especially high risk to you because if something happened to the mother skunk, and if that something happened to be dying of rabies, then there would be a good chance that her babies had contracted the disease from her. So be safe and just look but do not touch.

Just in case somebody gets careless, here's an off-the-shelf formula to chemically neutralize skunk spray that really works. This formula was sent to me years ago by a reader who clipped it from the letters to the editor column in a chemical engineering magazine. The sender unfortunately also clipped off the name of the writer and the magazine. All I know is that the writer was apparently a chemical engineer who cooked it up to deodorize his own skunked golden retriever. I don't have the engineer's name, but whoever the person is, he or she has my thanks and the blessings of thousands of pet owners over the years who can breathe again because of this chemical magic. (If you ever see this, my friend, please send me your name and address so we can communicate, and I will affix your name to this wonderful formula forevermore.)

De-Skunk Formula:

- 1 quart of 3 percent hydrogen peroxide (from a pharmacy)
- 1/4 cup baking soda
- 1 teaspoon liquid dish soap

Mix together ingredients and wash the skunk-sprayed animal, keeping the mixture out of its eyes, nose, and mouth. Rinse with tap water.

People who have tried the formula say this amount is enough for a small dog. Double it for medium-size dogs and triple it for large dogs.

You should use this stuff up immediately after mixing and don't try to bottle or store any leftovers for future use. The mixture causes a minor chemical reaction that produces expanding gases and lots of bubbles that could explode and make a big mess if confined to a bottle.

Eastern fox squirrel (*Sciurus niger*)

This is unverified, but I've been told by many different sources that Eastern fox squirrels were introduced into San Francisco's Golden Gate Park in the 1930s. What I do know for a fact is that they are now found about fifty miles from San Francisco in all directions (except west!).

Backyards are made for these reddish, fuzzy-tailed acrobats. These natural-born trapeze artists raid bird feeders and help themselves to plums, pears, apples, walnuts, almonds, and anything else in your yard that looks good. When they are not building their stick nests in treetops and attics (check those vent hole screens), these playful animals are usually doing cartwheels along fence tops and teasing the neighborhood dogs and cats.

One of my readers has a female Labrador retriever with one mission in life—to keep the squirrels out of *her* yard. They tease her unmercifully, running back and forth along the top of a six-foot fence, swishing their tails back and forth and chattering away at her.

One afternoon the dog's human was watching her interact with the squirrels when one of the squirrels dashed up a tree and out on a limb that stretched over the yard. As the dog stood on the ground directly under the squirrel, its human saw "a bright stream of something come from the area of the squirrel. It came down and hit the dog squarely on her head."

The squirrel had urinated onto the head of dog. A perfect shot!

Next time, may I suggest umbrellas at ten paces? I was once at a zoo listening to a docent lecture on primates in front of the chimpanzee cage. As he talked, a big male chimp climbed quietly up to the top front of the cage, directly above and behind the docent, took careful aim, and sent a "bright stream of something" at the man's head. At that exact instant, the tour guide whipped out a small umbrella from his rear pocket, snapped it open, and held it up just in time to divert the urine shower away from his head, all while he continued his lecture without ever looking back at the now screaming chimp.

Poetic.

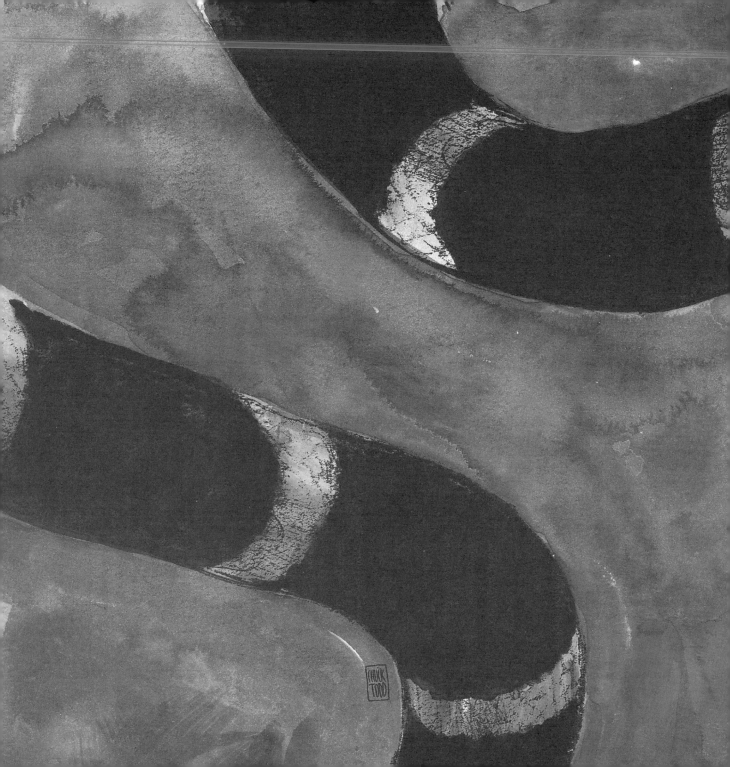

Reptiles

Reptiles always lose when their habitat is being developed by humans. There are no more rocky outcroppings for them to bask in the sun on, and a long trip across the road usually gets them squashed by speeding cars (ones that had probably aimed at them). A few of the more adaptable fence lizards and alligator lizards can survive and earn their keep in friendly neighborhood gardens. Snakes don't do well in yards, where many humans will unfortunately kill them when they see them. It is the humans' loss, however, because snakes, like all creatures, play an integral role in local ecosystems.

Coast garter snake
(Thamnophis elegans terrestris)

Garter snakes are usually found near streams and ponds, so look for them in similar spots in your yard. They feed on slugs they find under your garden vegetables, treefrogs and the mosquito fish in your backyard ornamental pond, and tiny mice when they can find them. Leave them alone (put down that hoe!) and they'll help you control the creatures that nibble on your garden plants.

Pacific gopher snake (Pituophis melanoleucus catenifer)

The Pacific gopher snake is one of the Bay Area's most common and attractive (yes, *attractive*) local snakes. It is a large yellowish or cream-colored snake with black or brown blotches down its back; its stomach is white to yellowish, often with black spots. It hisses loudly when angered. A frightened gopher snake flattens its head and vibrates its tail loudly in the dried leaves like a rattlesnake so you will leave it alone. This trick usually works.

Of the constrictor variety, it squeezes and smothers its prey, feeding on small mammals, birds, an occasional insect, lizards, frogs, toads, and other snakes. The amount of hunting territory a single gopher snake needs depends a lot on the availability of prey, but they probably need around an acre or less. Unfortunately for them, loss of habitat (we like to build houses in the fields where they hunt), too many cars (snakes are slaughtered on roads and highways across America), and the fact that they're always being mistaken for rattlesnakes (and then killed) has depleted their numbers over the years. Back in the "good old days" (translation: when I was a kid), I sometimes found gopher snakes that were four to five feet long. Now the very large and easy-to-spot snakes are getting harder and harder to find. At least, we don't often see them around the places where we live.

All snakes—even rattlesnakes—are an important and beneficial part of the local ecosystem. They eat all those things I mentioned earlier and are also a source of food themselves to other reptiles like the cannibalistic king snake, plus foxes, coyotes, raccoons, opossums, hawks, owls, and eagles. In the wild, animals like to invite other animals out to lunch—once.

You say you don't harm snakes because they control the "varmint" population in your yard? Does that mean you *would* harm snakes if there weren't any "varmints" around? Just curious. "Varmints" are usually in the eyes of the beholder, you know.

Slithery Gopher-Getters

One day thirty years ago, my neighbor's husband came home from work with a burlap sack. Inside were two large gopher snakes. She says he stuck each one down a gopher hole and for the rest of summer the garden flourished.

This may seem a sensible solution for a gopher problem, but it's actually not very humane for the gopher snake and it's certainly not a practical or efficient way to deal with gophers. Moving gopher snakes from the wild into the middle of town ends up getting them killed by cars, pets, and frightened homeowners. Putting one down a gopher hole is also no guarantee of a dead gopher. The snake is just as likely to crawl up out of another hole and across the street in front of a car without eating anything.

California king snake
(*Lampropeltis getulus californiae*)

These snakes, strikingly marked with alternating light and dark rings around their bodies, are usually very popular with us humans because, among other things, they also eat rattlesnakes when they encounter them. King snakes are immune to rattlesnake venom and kill their prey by constriction. They also eat other reptiles, small rodents,

birds, amphibians, and fish and they're nice to have around, whether you like snakes or not.

Northern Pacific rattlesnake
(*Crotalus viridis oreganus*)

Rattlers occasionally manage to crawl into town without getting run over by cars or chopped into pieces by somebody's shovel. You should make a note of this if you live near open spaces and/or have brush or rock piles in your yard that attract rodents and the poisonous rattlesnakes that like to eat them.

Pacific ringneck snake
(*Diadophis punctatus amabilis*)

Ringnecks are attractive reptiles about the size of a pencil that prowl through rotten logs and under your birdbath. They catch and eat slender salamanders, worms, and small insects. Cats will find these tiny gentle snakes and bring them home for their human parents to see. Please return them to a hiding place in your yard where they belong.

San Francisco alligator lizard
(*Gerrhonotus coeruleus coeruleus*)

Why do they call them alligator lizards? Because they look just like alligators, only six to eight inches long. You'll find them sunning in your garden or hunting for crickets, spiders, snails, etc.

Alligator lizards are just one of the many small (and not so small!) critters that crawl and slither around the house when we're not looking. A surprisingly large number of lizards (and Jerusalem crickets, cockroaches, spiders, and snakes) manage to squeeze in through the spaces under our kitchen doors. Tacking weather stripping on the bottom of the door helps to keep these insect and reptilian explorers outside where you think they belong, but if you have an indoor/outdoor cat, all bets are off. Cats seem to have a thing about collecting little "pets" and bringing them into the house to play with. Alligator lizards are a favorite.

You needn't worry about your reptilian visitor starving to death as it prowls around your house. An alligator lizard can go for months without eating because of its slow metabolism, but there are also usually plenty of tasty spiders and other small insects lurking under beds and furniture in the average house. A long stick (for poking behind furniture), a dust pan (for scooping up stray lizards), and a grocery sack (for transporting the lizard outside) should help you get rid of your unwanted visitor.

And they don't bite too hard, unless they get a small fold of skin. It's scary, though, if you've never been chomped by a lizard. Yes, they have teeth.

Oh yeah, the tail. The lizard can grow it back, but only once. Some lizards (including alligator lizards, fence lizards, and skinks) can "drop" their tails as a defense mechanism to keep from being eaten by predators. The tail muscles fit together like little fingers (clasp both your hands tightly together), and when something grabs the lizard's tail, these special muscles relax and separate (loosen your fingers and pull your hands apart). Other muscles clamp off blood vessels at the break point to stop the break from bleeding. Nerves are triggered to start the broken tail lashing and thrashing about to attract the predator's interest while the lizard escapes. Lizards can only use this special tail escape once. When the new tail grows back, all the muscles are of the normal non-release type.

Northwestern fence lizard (blue-belly) (*Sceloporus occidentalis occidentalis*)

The kids call these three- to six-inch lizards "blue-bellies" because of the blue markings on the sides of their bellies (and on the necks of the males). Don't let your cat catch and eat these lizards. Besides being extremely hard to digest (their hard, pointy scales can cause internal injuries to the cat), it's real tough on the lizards.

Western skink (*Eumeces skiltonianus*)

You will definitely know it when you spot a young Western skink slithering through your garden because they have bright metallic-blue tails. This is another one of the many lizard species that lose their tails as a defense mechanism—when they are grabbed by a predator, they can run away while the predator is busy eating the tail. Skink tails come off *very* easily, so just look and don't touch.

Northwestern pond turtle *(Clemmys marmorata marmorata)*

The olive-green Western pond turtle is a local native still found here and there, but it is a species of special concern in California because it is getting rarer every day due to pollution and loss of habitat. There are probably a lot more red-ear sliders and other imported pet-store turtles to be found in local creeks because that's where they usually get dumped when mom gets tired of cleaning their terrariums.

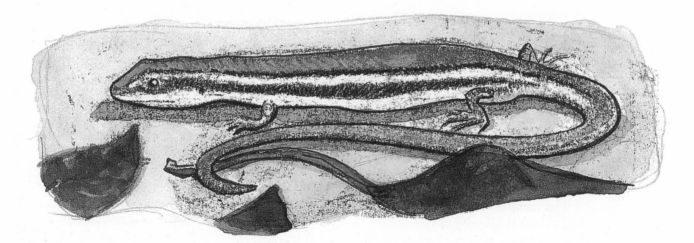

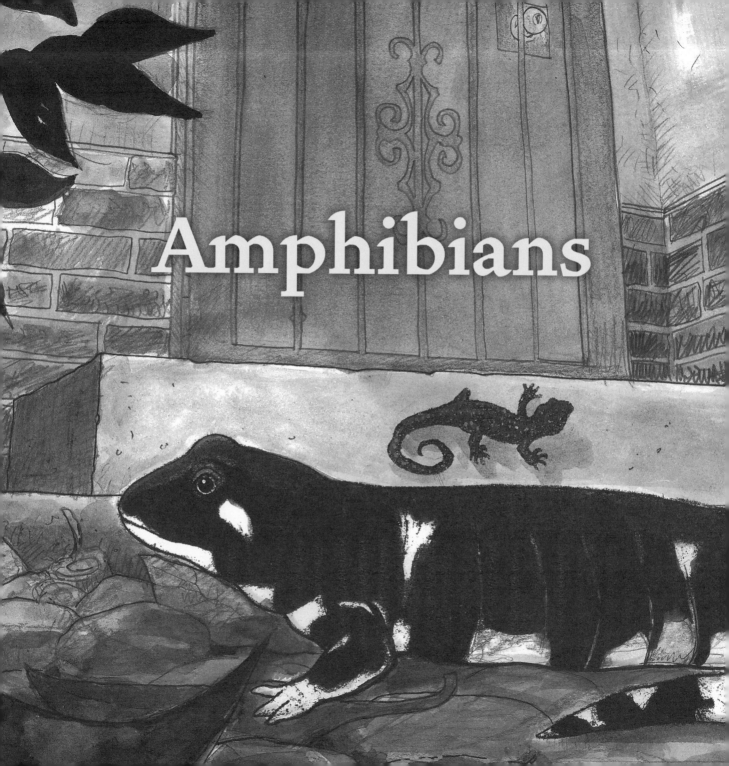

Amphibians

Amphibians need moisture, insects to feed on, a pond to breed and lay their eggs in, and a damp place to hide. A few species, like slender salamanders, Western toads, and Pacific treefrogs, survive in suburban and urban yards. If you spend a little time poking about, you might find them under rocks, woodpiles, and in the proximity of an occasional backyard pond. Sometimes you might even encounter a tiger salamander if you have a "natural" yard, but they are pretty rare and getting rarer all the time.

Pacific treefrog *(Hyla regilla)*

These brown-and-green amphibians hide in your garden and flowerpots. Sometimes they even sneak inside to live in your indoor plants and serenade you while you're watching television. They can change color from light to dark, making it harder for you to find them.

Have you ever heard the story about the 300-pound frog? When it croaks, even 300-pound canaries listen.

Most backyard a cappella choirs are made up of two-inch-long treefrogs. That's a far cry from the 300-pounder you expected, but they more than make up for their diminutive size with their incredibly, shall we say, "robust" voices. But for all their macho vocalizations, these tiny amphibians are actually very shy. The slightest noise (of an opening door) or vibration (of your feet stomping through the yard) will instantly silence them.

Alas, within minutes after you're back in bed, their industrious singing begins again. Personally, I like the sound of serenading treefrogs, although many other people don't. But I enjoy drifting off to sleep with that pleasant croaking in my ears, especially knowing they feed on many species of insects that are harmful to my garden, which means I don't have to use any nasty bug sprays.

Winter rains turn your yard into an amphibian wonderland. There are probably twenty to fifty treefrogs out there. Let's say half of them are males, and they're doing their darndest to attract the female treefrogs into hopping over and checking out their little voice boxes. You think you can shut those guys up?

We're talking amphibian sex here, folks. It's their rites, or rights (however you want to label it), of spring. Amphibian lust is hard to reason with, so forget it.

But I can still help you with your problem. Tear off the bottom of this page and divide it into two pieces. Wad them up and stuff one into each ear. Pleasant dreams.

California toad (Bufo boreas halophilus)

No, you can't get warts from touching a toad. Yes, they do have noxious skin secretions that make them taste bitter to dogs, raccoons, and anything else that tries to eat them. You will occasionally notice these portly amphibians waddling around your lawn in the evening, looking for any insect, spider, snail, or slug they can stuff into their huge mouths with their front feet.

Arboreal salamander (Aneides lugubris)

This is a five-inch amphibian that gets its name from its tree-climbing ability, aided by extra-long toes and a barely prehensile tail. They like to hide in moist places under loose bark, boards, and logs, and you can sometimes find these curious little salamanders lurking on the tops of porch lights at night, where they somehow manage to climb up to catch some of those fat, juicy moths attracted by the glow.

California slender salamander (Batrachoseps attenuatus)

Have you ever turned over a rock or a board and found what looks like a large earthworm with four tiny legs? Slender salamanders are one of the most common salamanders living in the Bay Area. You can put down this book and get up right now and go out in your backyard and turn over a rock or board or dig into some damp leaves and find one of these slick little guys wiggling around and eating *real* earthworms.

Coast range newt (Taricha torosa torosa)

South Park Drive in Tilden Regional Park (near Berkeley, California) is closed to vehicles from October to April so that thousands of these orange salamanders don't get flattened and mashed by cars when they migrate back and forth across the road to their breeding ponds. This species of newt secretes a neurotoxin from its skin that can paralyze or kill a small dog that eats it. Fortunately for the dog, they also taste extremely bitter and the dog usually spits them right back out again very quickly.

California tiger salamander (Ambystoma californiense)

These colorful six- to eight-inch-long salamanders used to be plentiful around the Bay Area, but in the last few decades populations have declined mainly because of loss of habitat due to human activity. They normally live in gopher and ground squirrel holes, but since we humans try like heck to get rid of gophers and ground squirrels, it makes it kind of rough on the salamanders. If you're lucky enough to find one, look and wonder, but leave it alone.

Tiny Wild Things

Jeepers, creepers, where'd they get those peepers
(and feelers)? Creeping, crawling, buzzing, stinging, burrowing,
web-slinging, sliming, hopping, pinching, rolling, munching, polli-
nating, egg-laying, and just downright infesting...these critters do
it all.

Put down that can of Raid and read on...

Monarch butterfly *(Danaus plexippus)*; anise swallowtail *(Papilio zelicaon)*

These are just two of the incredibly beautiful butter-fly species that you can often find flitting from flower to flower in your backyard. The swallowtail caterpillars feed on anise plants; monarch caterpil-lars munch on milkweed. Growing anise and milk-weed in your garden is a very good way to guarantee future visits from these delicate "living flowers."

Black saddlebags dragonfly *(Tramea lacerata)*

Fossil records indicate that dragonflies were buzzing about through the giant ferns and jungles of Carboniferous times over 300 million years ago, predating dinosaurs. No other insect can escape the high-speed maneuvers of these aerial predators.

They can't bite or sting humans, so sit back and enjoy their colorful antics as they zoom back and forth around you, catching mosquitoes in your yard.

Giant crane fly *(Holorusia rubiginosa)*

You really get noticed if you look like a giant mos-quito. Know what I mean? But you can relax because crane flies are actually quite harmless and don't even bite. On warm spring days and nights, these huge insects are suddenly everywhere,

banging into your screen doors and noisily thumping against the windows and being chased around the front room by your excited cats. Some people call them "mosquito hawks," but the adults rarely eat anything and are basically just egg-laying machines. This species is one of the largest flies in the world.

Western yellowjacket (*Vespula pensylvanica*)

As I'm sure you are very aware, yellowjackets aggressively protect their nests. Stepping on a nest or poking sticks down nest holes will quickly produce a loud swarm of agitated, stinging insects. Their natural enemies include skunks, who use their long front claws to dig up nests and feed on the larvae. This insect scavenger is a major pest that likes to fly around garbage cans and back patios when you barbecue during the summertime months.

But you might think twice before you decide to get rid of them because yellowjackets serve the environment as hunters, helping to keep fly and mosquito populations down. If they are buzzing around stinging you whenever you go out in your yard or have a barbecue, that's one thing. But if these insects are just *there,* then you might want to consider another option besides always just opting to kill them.

When I'm barbecuing and eating outside during the summer, I take a plate with a few pieces of whatever meat I'm barbecuing and put it out on the ground in the farthest reaches of my backyard. I do this well before we sit down to eat so the yellowjackets have already been attracted to the plate and are there eating the meat. With the exception of one or two stray yellowjackets who didn't get the message about the free meat on the plate, this usually works. Then, the yellowjackets get something to eat without being killed by the nasty humans, and the not-so-nasty humans get to dine in the yard without being bothered by the yellowjackets. And most important, the yellowjackets get to live in the yard and hunt flies and mosquitoes.

Give it a try and see what happens. You have nothing to lose and plenty to gain. If the insect populations take care of each other and keep things under control, that means you don't have to spray any noxious and potentially dangerous pesticides around your yard.

California carpenter bee (*Xylocopa californica*)

They're big, they're black, and they make a noisy buzz, but these bees are really quite gentle. They bore holes in wood where they lay eggs and leave pollen to feed their larvae. With wild honeybee populations decimated by years of mite infestations, carpenter bees (and bumblebees) have risen to the challenge to become important pollinators in our gardens.

If you don't like carpenter bees chewing holes in your beautiful new redwood fence, try making a carpenter bee condo. Just take a three-foot piece of 2" x 4" lumber, drill a lot of holes the same diameter as the natural carpenter bee holes you've seen (usually about a half an inch), and hang it up somewhere in your yard. The bees will take advantage of the free holes and hopefully leave your fence alone. I have a carpenter bee condo hanging over my patio. It makes a great conversation piece during my backyard barbecues.

"What's that?"

"That's where my carpenter bees live."

"Oh."

Sow bug *(Porcellio scaber)*; pill bug *(Armadillium vulgare)*

For as long as I can remember, kids have called sow bugs "roly-poly bugs" or "pill bugs" because they roll up into armor-plated balls after being disturbed. It may surprise you to learn that these terrestrial crustaceans are actually two different look-alike creatures. They are not the same bug at all. The main difference between them is that pill bugs can roll into a ball and sow bugs can't. Both feed mostly on decaying vegetation and occasionally on young plants.

European earwig *(Forficula auricularia)*

These "pincher bugs" hide under or in everything, even inside the spaces of your rolled-up morning newspaper. People fear them because of the huge forceps (pincers) on the tip of the male's abdomen (used in defense and in courtship displays) and even the tiny pincers on the females, but they can't pinch very hard.

These non-native insects *can* be seriously destructive to certain plants and flowers in your garden. They can also be, believe it or not, beneficial because they are omnivorous and also eat other insects. Few native creatures will eat earwigs because they smell and taste *very* bad. Don't believe me? Go ahead and sniff one and you'll see what I mean. (Watch out for those pincers!)

Hornworm moth *(Manduca sexta)*

There's nothing quite like the chomp, chomp, chomp of a tomato hornworm masticating its rubbery way through your precious tomato patch. Green zebras, Early Girls, Big Boys, Romas, and Sweet 100s, all fall before the mighty jaws of this giant larva that resembles Jabba the Hut of *Star Wars* fame. Who would have guessed that fat green "thing" would encase itself in a nondescript pupa, undergo a magical metamorphosis, and finally emerge as a beautiful, fragile flying creature—a lovely sphinx moth?

Black and yellow argiope spider (*Argiope aurantia*)

The argiope spider is one of several species of arachnids we call garden spiders. They spin huge, wondrous round webs in our yards and gardens. All are nonpoisonous to humans (but all insects beware!). It is good to recognize their special space in your garden. An angry spider can really mess up your day when you're bending over your tomatoes.

Spider in Winter

The rain crashed against the sliding glass door to my home office like waves roiling the surface of a tide pool. I stood there, my nose pressed against the fogged glass, trying to see what was going on in my backyard as rivulets of water made everything wavy and unreal. The first heavy rainstorms of fall are always the most exciting ones of all. The sound, like the patter of millions of little running feet, is invigorating and full of unbridled energy. When it comes at night and the wind and water pound on my windows, I'm somehow always awake and filled with thoughts. Only I can never seem to remember what they were. Just thoughts. But I know they must have been good because when I finally go to sleep it's always the best sleep I ever had. Sound familiar?

If I squinted real hard I could see through the glass as if I were looking through the fisheye lens of a camera. Everything was distorted. The roses shivered and their thorny branches shook as the wind and rain battered the remaining petals from the nearly spent blooms and sprinkled the green lawn with red and yellow and pink and white and purple scales.

Amazingly, Arabella the argiope garden spider was still there, clad in her fancy duds, all eight legs set valiantly astride a huge bucking web that stretched all the way from the pole beans to a green zebra tomato plant. The fat raindrops tore great rents in her sturdy web—a meteor shower heralding the end of the world as she once knew it.

But the spider was undaunted. She scurried from one hole to another, pausing to make her instant repairs with a spindly leg that yanked out a long silken lasso from her spinnerets and snared and bound the broken sides together with magical spidery knots.

I couldn't stand it any longer and I went out into the garage and pulled on my yellow rubber pants and the yellow rubber coat with the big hood and my wife's bright red rubber boots (hey, they were the only ones I could find!)—and then I sloshed out into the yard like a giant fancy songbird with glandular problems. (Eat your heart out, *Sesame Street*!)

And so who was the first creature I met while I was out on my soggy stroll? My backyard's resident male Anna's hummingbird, sitting primly on his power branch on the apple tree. We both stood there staring at each other. Me admiring the intensity of his blood-red chin patch as it shimmered in the dim light of the storm, and him cocking his head and checking out my fancy bright red boots.

They'll never fit, I snickered, and I'll swear he looked me in the eye and stuck out his very long tongue. Birds, especially the tiniest ones, can be amazingly pushy.

All around us the storm was splattering the air with gusts of wind that ripped the yellowing leaves from the trees and threw them on the ground. The rising water was churning dirt into mud and drowning all the snails I was never able to catch all summer and lapping against my boots as the rain slapped my face with a million fingers.

But the hummer just sat there, calm and dry and completely unruffled in his private little eye of the storm. I wiped a cold drop of water off my nose and sniffed. It's not fair, you know. Mother Nature likes him best.

In the distance, I could hear the ringing of a telephone calling me back to reality. On the way to the house, I veered over by the vegetable garden and looked around. Arabella the garden spider, and her web, were gone...forever.

Bay Area blond tarantula (*Aphonopelma smithi*)

In the fall, large numbers of these monster spiders, mostly the males, will stroll back and forth across the roads and hills of Mount Diablo, seeking sexy spider women. If they are lucky, each will find a beautiful lady spider who will mate with him, and then kill and eat him for dinner. Strange relationship.

Regardless of the terrible things you have seen these big spiders do in the monster tarantula movies, they are actually quite gentle creatures. The bites of Bay Area species are about as painful as a bee sting. Tropical tarantulas, however, are another, more painful story.

Western black widow (*Latrodectus hesperus*)

Poisonous black widow spiders are commonly found hiding in dark, quiet places in most yards throughout California. They live under your house or under the rocks and board piles in yards. The female widow is easily recognized by her glossy black body, spindly legs, and the hard-to-see orange-red hourglass-shaped spot under her abdomen. The tiny, light-colored male is usually nearby but he can't bite you. Black widow webs are among the strongest in the spider world.

Garden snail (*Helix aspersa*); spotted garden slug (*Limax maximus*)

A slug is a kind of snail without a shell. Slugs and snails both eat all kinds of plant materials, especially (surprise!) the plants that grow in your garden, and then recycle them back into the soil. Snails and slugs are also an important food source for fish, birds, and some species of mammals and reptiles that will eat just about anything. That includes opossums, skunks, raccoons, scrub jays, and garter snakes. Human gardeners, of course, hate them for some reason.

Jerusalem cricket
(Stenopelmatus fuscus)

Behind that scary demeanor is actually a very useful critter because the big, shiny, and very Kafkaesque "potato bugs" prey on lots of other insects. They roam around our yards at night and get into our houses (usually by squeezing under the crack at the bottom of your back door) and frighten the heck out of people. They can nip pretty hard with those big, imposing mandibles (or, as I called them when I was a kid, "CHOMPERS!"), but they are in fact quite harmless to humans. Honest.

California common scorpion
(Paruroctonus silvestrii)

There are several subspecies of small scorpions living throughout the San Francisco Bay Area, but we rarely see them because they live under things and only come out to prowl and hunt at night. Their stings are relatively harmless, unless you or your pets are allergic to the venom. Some scorpion species found in other desert areas, states, and countries are poisonous. These helpful creatures spend a lot of time hunting and keeping backyard insect populations in check. Take a deep breath and leave them alone.

How to Be a Good Tiny Wild Thing Neighbor

Do you really have to spray pesticides around your yard? Did you know that more pesticides are sprayed in backyards than are used by farmers in their fields? That's kind of scary.

When you spray pesticides to kill flies or mosquitoes or yellowjackets, you are also killing lots of other beneficial insects and arachnids, like butterflies, moths, and spiders. If this is important to you, and it should be, take some time to turn on your computer and do an Internet search for "less lethal pest control." You will hopefully be delighted to discover that there are plenty of ways to get along with the insects you consider to be tiny wild pests without having to kill them.

Exotic Wildlife

Escaped Exotic Pets and Other Strange Beasts

It is pretty common for you to find non-native wild creatures poking around in your yard or garbage these days. Some of your neighbors collect boa constrictors, parrots, ferrets, and probably lots of other exotic wild animals you'd never heard of except on the Discovery Channel—until you found one of "those things" slithering, hopping, crawling, or flying around your patio. Or in your garage; for some reason, escaped exotic pets *really* like to hide in garages. That's where I found a wallaby one time in Orinda.

What do you do when you find one? Call animal control and then go get your camera.

Emu *(Dromaius novaehollandiae)*

Some days, the East Bay looks like it's part of the Australian outback. Between 1998 and 2002, eight Australian emus were spotted jogging around the cities of Danville, Alamo, Livermore, Pittsburg, and Concord. These five-foot-tall, 150-pound, flightless, ostrich-like birds were all escaped pets. They run thirty to forty miles per hour, have a powerful kick like a mule, and can do serious damage to humans and dogs with their sharp claws. A birdkeeper friend at a local zoo affectionately refers to his emus as "velociraptors," and zookeepers around the world have been kicked and scarred by these fast, aggressive, territorial birds.

Budgerigar (parakeet) *(Melopsittacus undulatus)*; scarlet macaw *(Ara macao)*

Every year when it gets warm and people leave their doors and windows open, parakeets, scarlet macaws, all sorts of exotic parrots and cockatoo species, and other non-native birds escape from careless owners and fly off into the skies of the urban and suburban wilderness. One summer, I estimated that $50,000 worth of exotic pet birds were fluttering around and screaming in the East Bay. I'm sure it was the same in other areas around California and the rest of the country wherever these birds are popular as pets. Some people just can't resist parading around with their birds on their arms, and many of the people who do this also forget to keep the wing feathers clipped short enough so the birds can't fly away and eventually starve to death, get caught by predators, catch some disease, or freeze to death during the winter months. Because of mild winters around the San Francisco Bay Area, these exotics will sometimes survive for years, feeding at backyard bird feeders and on fruit trees.

Peacock *(Pavo cristatus)*

In the 1970s, about sixty-five peafowl lived in the retirement community of Rossmoor at the south end of the city of Walnut Creek. Every spring, the peahens raised large families of peachicks, while the peacocks screamed their fool heads off (a truly awesome sound, especially at 5 a.m.).

A few of the chicks always struck out to explore the world beyond Rossmoor's guarded gates, and eventually there were feral peacocks living all around the East Bay. They still show up today. (The noise finally ruffled too many Rossmoor residents' feathers and most of the original peacock colony were caught and sent to live on some farms in the country.)

Ringneck dove *(Streptopelia risoria)*

This is probably the most common domestic dove being kept in captivity. They have reportedly been bred by bird-loving humans for more than two thousand years, and the large number of ringnecks that have escaped from backyard aviaries over the years have continued to breed in the wild. This dove species comes in gray and white and they like to dine on seeds with flocks or pairs of the native mourning doves that visit and build their nests in your yard.

European ferret *(Mustela furo)*

At the time this book was written, these domesticated weasels were legal pets in all states except Hawaii and California. But despite the ban, there are still anywhere from an estimated 100,000 to 500,000 (depending on who you're talking to) illegal pet ferrets living in California with their humans. Ferret-lovers have been trying for years to pass laws to make their pets legal, but the California Department of Fish and Game has successfully fought them, claiming that non-native pet ferrets would create havoc in the state's ecosystem if they escaped, survived, and became established in the wild. While there have been large numbers of ferrets kept as pets in California for more than thirty years (and probably longer), that scenario has yet to happen.

Coatimundi *(Nasua narica)*

This raccoon-like animal has a slighter build, a long and semi-prehensile tail, and a long, flexible snout that wiggles around in the air and sticks out quite a way over its lower lip. They are native to Texas, Arizona, Mexico, and Central and South America, but pet owners from states where these mammals can be kept legally sometimes bring them illegally into California when they move. These clever creatures often escape from their cages and are what belong to that funny-looking nose that occasionally pokes through your cat door.

California desert tortoise *(Gopherus agassizii)*

One reason these gentle vegetarians have become endangered is because people collect them while visiting the desert on vacation, bring them home, and release them to live in their backyards. Once these heat-loving desert reptiles wake up from hibernation, they dig out under back fences and can be found roaming up and down the streets looking for the desert. They often wander through open garage doors and under workbenches (one actually climbed through a cat door!) and are discovered cuddling up to warm clothes dryers.

Colombian boa constrictor
(Boa constrictor imperator)

Colombian boas can grow to be twelve feet long, but the pet store snakes are usually from twelve inches to six feet long when you buy them. They're called "red-tailed boas" because they have reddish-brown tail markings.

It often seems as if every kid on the block has had a pet boa at one time or another, and it's fairly common to discover these harmless (except to small cats and pet rats) escaped pets in your garage or yard. Just toss a beach towel over it so it can't bite you, drop everything in a pillowcase, and go knock on some doors up and down the street until you find the owner. They don't crawl very far.

American alligator
(Alligator mississippiensis)

Our most famous local escaped gator had to be the San Francisco Presidio's Mountain Lake Gator. In the fall of 1996, while the *San Francisco Chronicle* was hiring an alligator hunter to catch it (so they could have fun writing about it!) and the competing newspaper's editor was threatening to do the job himself in his wetsuit (so *his* newspaper could write about it), a San Francisco Zoo curator, John Aiken, caught the three-foot reptile all by himself. (Most escaped pet alligators are under three feet long; much bigger than that and their humans have trouble handling them.)

There have been reports of "huge" alligators in local reservoirs (actually logs) and the Delta sloughs (lines of mallard ducks zig-zagging through the water), but nothing verified—yet.

Green iguana (Iguana iguana)

There are either a lot of pet green iguanas in Martinez, California, or maybe just one clever and very fast escapee.

"Hello, Police? I want to report a four-foot green dragon sunning itself on the sidewalk in front of the Wells Fargo Bank!" "Hello, Police? There's a four-foot green lizard in my garden." "Hello, Police? There's a big green dragon running down the street!"

Pet stores sell them, and they have become a huge problem in Florida where many have escaped to become established in warm local swamps. These harmless vegetarian lizards can cause serious injuries with their razor-sharp claws and thrashing tails if you try to catch them, so be careful.

Better to go knock on nearby doors to see who lost the magic green dragon.

Wild Neighbors
of the Future

As we human beasties hunger for more open space to accommodate our continually growing needs, there are bound to be more and more interesting encounters with wildlife in suburban and urban settings in the future. And there will be all the old regulars, of course, which you've been reading about in this book. Keep in mind that I've only just touched the surface here, taking a quick look with you at just a few of the animals that you might encounter in your backyard. Human interactions with some of these wild creatures could be increasing in the future, whether we like it or not, and attempts may have to be made to resolve this potential problem. We'll just have to wait and see, won't we?

Here are some thoughts, ideas, projections, predictions, and theories about the kinds of wild neighbors you may have moving in next door to you in the future.

Be sure to invite them over for dinner after they move in, to try and get things started off on the right foot, paw, or whatever.

Mammals ....

Coyotes *(Canis latrans)*

Coyote populations seem to have been growing throughout the East Bay over the last ten years or so. This correlates with the increase of housing developments in the area at the same time. I see no reason for this to change, at least in the immediate future. Coyote populations tend to depend a lot on the availability of food sources, so these predators should increase right along with any new development. Since the coyotes I'm talking about have adapted quite well to living in suburban and urban situations by raiding garbage cans and eating a seemingly endless supply of pet cats, as well as an occasional dog, I don't expect them to suddenly go away. We humans aren't going away either, nor are our pets.

Prediction: I expect the encounters between coyotes, humans, and especially our pets to increase in the future. Some county or state agency will eventually have to deal with the pet loss in response to increasing complaints from pet owners, especially if some of the coyotes get tamer and more daring (two miniature schnauzers were snatched off an Orinda front lawn by two coyotes in 1999), but I don't expect it to be anything more than a token response for political purposes.

Federal wildlife officials started a national trapping program in this country to try to wipe out coyotes around 1915. Since then federal trappers and ranchers have killed hundreds of thousands of coyotes in the United States. Just in 1999, approximately eight thousand coyotes were killed in the state of Oregon alone.

And what has been the end result of all this trapping, poisoning, and shooting of coyotes? Conservationists say that coyote populations have flourished and there are more of them now than ever. Predators that live in a good habitat tend to respond to pressures on their populations biologically by increasing their reproduction rate and having more young per litter. There are certainly more coyotes than there were when the feds decided to start wiping them out. Hmmm. There's a moral lurking around here someplace—maybe it's hiding in the bushes with the coyotes.

Black bears (Ursus americanus)

A news story filed by Knight Ridder Newspapers on July 26, 2000, reported that there were "an estimated 25,000 to 35,000 black bears in California" according to the state Department of Fish and Game—"a significant increase from the past few decades." And because the expanding populations of both bears and humans need somewhere to go, there are bound to be more interactions in the future.

In October 2000, an adult black bear entered a residential neighborhood in Folsom. That bear tipped over a few garbage cans, awakened a few noisy dogs, and headed back to the hills. A local police officer reported it was the first time he had heard of a bear in the town during the twenty-six years he had been working on the Folsom police force.

In 2002, another black bear that had come into town to raid garbage cans was treed by state game wardens in the city of Carmel, California. The poor bear fell seventy feet to its death after being hit with a tranquilizer dart. A few months later, about twenty miles away from Carmel in Salinas, yet another black bear found wandering the city was successfully captured and released back into the wild.

And in June 2003, a small black bear was spotted going through garbage cans at Point Reyes National Seashore, just north of San Francisco. A ranger said it was the first bear sighting at the park in more than one hundred years. The bear hasn't been seen again, but automatic cameras have been set up to record the event in case the bear returns.

Prediction: If you live anywhere near what is popularly known as "bear country," I suggest you make sure your garbage can lids are secure and bear proof from now on.

Wolves *(Canis lupus)*

There is talk of reintroducing wolves into the Northern California wilderness.

Prediction: That would be interesting...

Wild turkeys *(Meleagris gallopavo)*

Wild turkey populations are going to continue to grow now that the ravenous turkeys have discovered the giant suburban barnyard formerly known as the San Francisco Bay Area. Pretty soon we're going to have a wild turkey sitting on every rooftop. (On Thanksgiving, we'll have to serve corn on the cob with tofu to keep from hurting their feelings.)

Prediction: A big bird told me that government wildlife agencies are starting to get so many complaints that they are going to have to do something about the overpopulation. This is ironic because wild turkeys were introduced into California as game birds by the Department of Fish and Game in the first place. I have been told by a friend in the DFG that options under consideration at the time this book went to press included relocating the problem turkeys and/or killing them.

It is currently against state law in California to relocate depredating wild animals because they could spread local diseases to or otherwise disrupt the resident wild turkeys in the new area. Nevertheless, this may be the best solution considering that the other option is killing the turkeys.

These big, beautiful birds, which Ben Franklin once nominated over the bald eagle as the symbol of our country, are also becoming quite popular with a large segment of the local human residents in communities where they are starting to gobble. It could turn into a huge public relations disaster for any agency that approves and promotes the killing of Ben Franklin's favorite bird. Stay tuned.

Reptiles and Amphibians ....

Reptiles and amphibians have a lot of problems in the urban and suburban wilderness. They get run over by cars, eaten by cats, and killed by dogs and humans.

Prediction: With the decrease of their natural habitat, snakes and lizards are going to continue to get rarer and rarer and rarer...

Prediction: With the decrease of their natural habitat, salamanders, newts, frogs, and toads are going to continue to get rarer and rarer and rarer...

Even Stranger Exotics ....

Parrots

Amazon parrots, cockatoos of all types, macaws, African grays, and other exotic birds are getting more and more popular every day, and I expect a growing stream of escaped exotic pet birds to continue to fill the skies like an explosion of feathery skyrockets on the Fourth of July.

Prediction: The only way this problem will end is if animal dealers stop selling exotic birds. I don't see that happening unless they run out of exotic birds, and that, of course, would mean there would be no more exotic birds left in the wild to be caught and sold in the worldwide and not-always-legal animal trade.

Big cats

In October 2000, four 600- to 800-pound African lions were shot while they were wandering near the central Arkansas community of Quitman. They were believed to have some connection to a nearby exotic animal farm. According to the Associated Press story on the incident, "Residents say the terror may not be over, because no one knows for sure whether more lions are on the loose." Are there any exotic animal farms near where you live? It sure wouldn't hurt to find out what kinds of exotic animals they're farming.

Even though the names and faces of the creatures may change in the future, people will still be excited to see or have anything to do with their wild neighbors. Some may consider certain animals, like the wild turkeys, as pests, but most people will be thrilled to have any interaction with them. Some things never change.

Epilogue ....

Bumping heads with wild animals is a problem that isn't going to go away. Loss of wild habitat has been causing conflicts between man and beast in this country ever since some pilgrim built the first log cabin atop a gopher hole, and it has only gotten worse as we land-hungry humans usurp more and more wildlife habitat and reshape it to our own plastic, steel, and concrete designs.

Annually, raccoons damage or destroy hundreds, maybe even thousands of lawns around the Bay Area. Deer that once lived on the slopes and browsed in the grassy valleys around Mount Diablo now sleep in suburban yards and munch on our roses. We grumble and complain if they damage our lawns and gardens, but we get frightened and understandably vengeful if the injury is to one of us or to a loved one. Then it becomes personal. But let's remember to be scientific and compassionate and humane and realistic about it.

When the populations of certain wild species dwindle to a precious few, some may need to be objectively managed and nurtured and cultivated in ways that ensure their continued survival in their wild, free, and natural state. And to do that, we need copious quantities of wide open spaces. No populated suburb or busy inner-city neighborhood is even remotely capable of supporting as much biodiversity as the plain old natural open spaces that existed here before we humans came along and despoiled it.

The wild creatures that live in the urban wilderness are not the same as the wild creatures that live in the natural wilderness away from humans. They don't eat the same food, drink from the same streams, climb the same trees, den in the same hollows, build their nests from the same materials, or interact with humans in the same way as normal wild animals do. Although they may look alike, remember that they are not the same, at least not in their heads or habits.

Not all species can survive in the urban wilderness, and those that do are probably changed forever. Is this what we have to look forward to in the future as the last remaining open spaces shrink to postage stamp–size plots? If we are to keep a healthy, viable wild population of all the animals found in the natural, undeveloped environment, there have to be adequate wild spaces to support the complete range of biological diversity. In the best of all worlds, there should even be large protected areas where man and wildlife do not ever mix.

But don't get me wrong. It's nice to see wildlife living in the city. I enjoy feeding the birds from my backyard feeders like everyone else, and it's fun to spot a turkey vulture gliding over my house and a skunk waddling down the street when I leave for work in the morning. But is it really a good thing that these wild animals live here, in such close proximity to humans? It is simply not natural for some of these animals to have these kinds of interactions.

The wild animals that presently live in our artificial suburban and urban wilderness offer us a unique opportunity to study and observe them. And I really think we should do this, and not just in a casual, random, conversational way like I've done in this book. We need biologists and ecologists and other scientists to look into these unique backyard relationships that are going on around where we live so we can find out what happens to all these different wild species when we move into their natural habitats and reshape them for our own use.

Is my little unscientific peek into the habits of the different kinds of wild creatures that live among us just a hint of some of the many subtle, unknown, and not-so-nice ways we may be affecting their daily lives? Is it going to get worse as our human populations (and needs) grow and our ravenous appetites for more land and resources increase by leaps and bounds? What of diseases that might pass back and forth between creatures of the natural and the urban wilderness? Are those never-ending open spaces going to be—gasp—gone some day (a thought so shocking I didn't even want to say it)?

As we participate in the laborious process of trying to figure all this out, we also need to take a long, careful look at how we humans manage ourselves. Otherwise, we may well become one with the very beasts we are trying to save. And if that happens, what new wilderness will we humans find ourselves forced to live in, and who (or what) will try to save *us*?

A Final Thought

I don't want this book to end on a depressing note, okay? As long as our wild neighbors live here, we should enjoy them.

My wife, Lois, and I go for walks together every weekend in the city of Benicia, where we live. We go looking for new worlds. We also hold hands when we walk. You should try it. It makes you feel young.

Benicia, like most spots where we humans choose to live, is a city of nooks and crannies. There are the neatest little places to find around every corner: tiny gnome houses covered by growing things with just the windows showing through to let in some light, beautiful cactus gardens to transport you to a desert canyon. And of course the wild creatures that are always hopping, slithering, crawling, and fluttering around for you to see—if you bother to look.

Where would a city be without its wildlife? (Where would the wildlife be without the city?)

Earlier this year it was the robins—they were everywhere. Huge flocks of fifty to eighty birds (I tried to count them; forget it!), chirping into the sky and landing halfway down the next block to completely envelop a little brown house and all the trees around it. We saw one bush that sparkled in the morning sun with dozens of red-breasted berries. It seemed like every robin in the Bay Area was visiting Benicia that day. I hope they enjoyed their stay. We certainly did.

I especially remember a potted fern we saw on one walk. It was covered with tiny green treefrogs. Real, *live* treefrogs. And there was the sidewalk in front of one old house with all the alligator lizards skittering through the fallen leaves. What a great old house! We stop and look at the lizards whenever we pass.

Whether it's Benicia, Walnut Creek, or the town where you live anywhere in the United States or the world, you should take a walk with your sweetie this weekend and discover who and what your wild neighbors are.

And don't forget to hold hands. Lois and I think that's the best part.

Sizing Up the Neighborhood ....

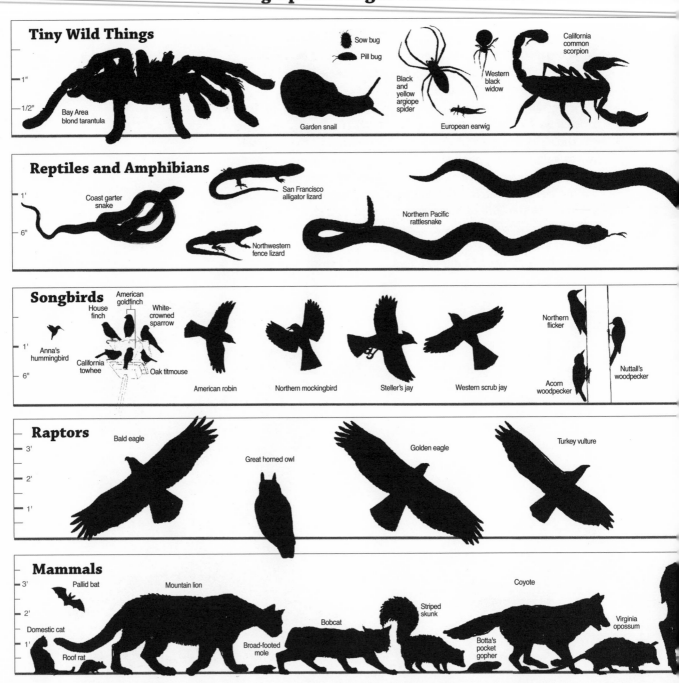

Tiny Wild Things

1"

1/2"

Bay Area blond tarantula

Garden snail

Sow bug

Pill bug

Black and yellow argiope spider

Western black widow

California common scorpion

European earwig

Reptiles and Amphibians

1'

6"

Coast garter snake

San Francisco alligator lizard

Northwestern fence lizard

Northern Pacific rattlesnake

Songbirds

American goldfinch

House finch

White-crowned sparrow

1'

6"

Anna's hummingbird

California towhee

Oak titmouse

American robin

Northern mockingbird

Steller's jay

Western scrub jay

Northern flicker

Acorn woodpecker

Nuttall's woodpecker

Raptors

3'

2'

1'

Bald eagle

Great horned owl

Golden eagle

Turkey vulture

Mammals

3'

2'

1'

Pallid bat

Mountain lion

Domestic cat

Roof rat

Broad-footed mole

Bobcat

Striped skunk

Botta's pocket gopher

Coyote

Virginia opossum

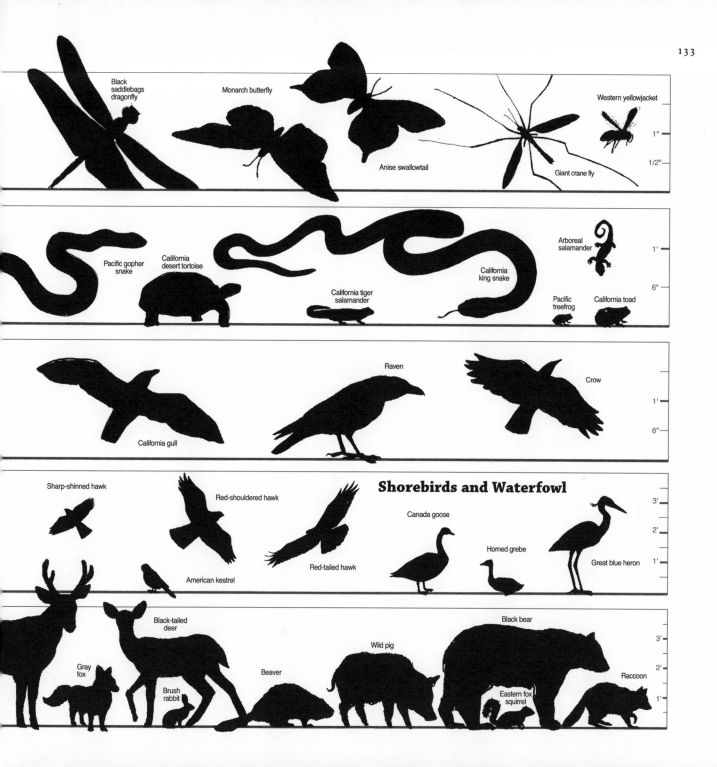

Black saddlebags dragonfly

Monarch butterfly

Anise swallowtail

Giant crane fly

Western yellowjacket

1"

1/2"

Pacific gopher snake

California desert tortoise

California tiger salamander

California king snake

Arboreal salamander

Pacific treefrog

California toad

1'

6"

California gull

Raven

Crow

1'

6"

Sharp-shinned hawk

Red-shouldered hawk

Shorebirds and Waterfowl

Canada goose

Horned grebe

Great blue heron

American kestrel

Red-tailed hawk

3'

2'

1'

Gray fox

Black-tailed deer

Brush rabbit

Beaver

Wild pig

Black bear

Eastern fox squirrel

Raccoon

3'

2'

1'

List of Illustrations ....

Appendix: Friends of the Urban Wilderness

Wildlife Rescue Organizations ....

There are special organizations that assist urban and suburban wild creatures when they get into trouble. These include nonprofit groups dedicated to wildlife care, like natural history museums, SPCAs, and local humane societies; local, state, and federal agencies, like city and county animal control departments, the state Fish and Game Department and the U.S. Fish and Wildlife Service; and nonprofit land trusts.

There are two professional wildlife rehabilitator organizations in the United States: the International Wildlife Rehabilitation Council (IWRC) and the National Wildlife Rehabilitators Association (NWRA). If you are interested in this field, check out these organizations' Web sites at www.iwrc-online.org and www.nwrawildlife.org

If you find an injured or orphaned wild animal, call your local wildlife care center for advice. If you don't know where it is, check with a nearby natural history museum, veterinarian, city or county animal control shelter, humane society, SPCA, or state or federal wildlife agency and ask them to refer you to the nearest wildlife care center.

You can also go online and visit the IWRC Web site (see above) and click on the red button labeled "Wildlife Emergency." You will find a complete list of suggestions on how to temporarily care for the animal you've found until you can get it some professional help. Do not, please, try to care for the injured or orphaned wild animal yourself. This is a job for experienced veterinarians and trained volunteers who know how to properly care for these wild creatures until they can be released back into the wild. If you try to do it yourself (which is illegal in most states), you can (and probably will) end up killing the animal or, at the very least, keep it from being released back into the wild where it belongs. As far as a wild animal is concerned, that is probably worse than death. There is also the risk of you or your pets picking up a disease or parasite if you try to keep a wild animal in your home and care for it.

Thanks for caring...and for doing it right.

Nonprofit Wildlife Care Organizations ....

There are hundreds of wildlife care centers all across the country. Some are small and operated by a few paid staff members and teams of trained volunteers with medical help donated by veterinarians in the community. The wild animals being cared for are usually treated as outpatients and kept in special cages and aviaries constructed at the homes of volunteers. A few of the larger centers have their own in-house facilities to hold animals that are being treated.

Lindsay Wildlife Museum

1931 First Avenue, Walnut Creek, CA 94597; 925-935-1978; www.wildlife-museum.org

Mission Statement: Lindsay Wildlife Museum connects people with wildlife to inspire responsibility and respect for the world we share.

The Lindsay Wildlife Museum was founded in 1955. It operates the oldest and one of the largest professional wildlife rehabilitation centers in the country. Today, the museum's wildlife hospital, full-time veterinarian, veterinary technicians, staff, and hundreds of volunteers care for more than six thousand injured and orphaned wild animals every year. Most are brought to them by concerned local residents who find the animals in their yards or on the side of the road while driving to work.

The museum also has a large display of non-releasable local wild animals for public viewing so that you can see some of your wild neighbors up close and personal.

International Bird Rescue Research Center

Headquarters in Northern California: San Francisco Oiled Wildlife Care and Education Center, 4369 Cordelia Road, Fairfield, CA 94534; 707-207-0380; www.ibrrc.org

IBRRC in Southern California: Los Angeles Oiled Bird Care and Education Center, 3601 South Gaffey Street, San Pedro, CA 90731; 310-514-2573

Mission Statement: The International Bird Rescue Research Center is dedicated to mitigating the human impact on aquatic birds and other wildlife, worldwide. This is achieved through emergency response, education, research, and planning.

Nonprofit Land Trusts ....

Regional nonprofit land trusts are the ultimate friends of the urban wilderness. These organizations work to preserve the last remaining vital open spaces before they are developed. They also attempt to find and save corridors that link the open spaces. Without these protected natural lands and the corridors between them, many of the wild animals that live in our communities would not be able to travel from open space area to open space area. This is vital to species that need to interact and breed with other animals of the same species.

Save Mount Diablo

1196 Boulevard Way, Suite 10, Walnut Creek, CA 94595; 925-947-3535; www.savemountdiablo.org

Mission Statement: To secure through acquisition, protection, and preservation, the open space necessary to support the full range of biological diversity and to insure the integrity of Mount Diablo's natural beauty.

Muir Heritage Land Trust

P.O. Box 2452, Martinez, CA 94553; 925-228-5460; www.muirheritagelandtrust.org

Mission Statement: The Muir Heritage Land Trust works to ensure a lasting quality of life for future generations by preserving and stewarding open space and fostering environmental awareness.

Other Local, State, and Federal Agencies ......

California Department of Fish and Game

1416 Ninth Street, Sacramento, CA 95814; 916-445-0411; www.dfg.ca.gov

Mission Statement: The mission of the Department of Fish and Game is to manage California's diverse fish, wildlife, and plant resources, and the habitats upon which they depend, for their ecological values and for their use and enjoyment by the public.

Contra Costa Animal Services Department

Martinez Shelter: 4849 Imhoff Place, Martinez, CA 94553; 925-646-2995; www.ccasd.org

Pinole Shelter: 651 Pinole Shores Drive, Pinole, CA 94564; 510-374-3966

Animal Services officers transport injured and orphaned wildlife to the Lindsay Wildlife Museum for treatment and care until they can be released back into the wild.

United States Fish and Wildlife Service

Pacific Region Offices: 1633 Bayshore Highway, Suite 248, Burlingame, CA 94010; 650-876-9078; http://pacific.fws.gov.

Mission Statement: Working with others to conserve, protect, and enhance fish, wildlife, and plants and their habitats for the continuing benefit of the American people.

Contra Costa Wildlife Advisory Committee

Meets regularly at the Contra Costa County Public Works Department Road Maintenance Division Squad Room, 2475 Waterbird Way, Martinez, CA; 925-335-1230; www.co.contra-costa.ca.us/depart/cd/water/FWC

Mission Statement: Advise the Board of Supervisors on fish and wildlife issues that may affect Contra Costa County (CCC); make recommendations to the Board for the expenditure of funds from the fish and game Wildlife Propagation Fund pursuant to Fish and Game Code Section 13103; address issues surrounding the enforcement of fish and game laws and regulations in CCC; and consider other issues referred to the Committee by the Board.

Where You Live ....

The organizations listed above are just a few of the friends of the urban wilderness that exist in California and operate in the San Francisco Bay Area, where most of the events listed in this book occurred. You can find many more similar organizations in your own community. The names may be changed slightly, or even dramatically, but the things they do and their mission statements are basically the same. Seek them out if you need their services. Support them in what they do, with monetary donations, by volunteering and helping them with their work, by donating materials they might need, or just by being there when they need you. We humans and our wild neighbors are all creatures of the urban wilderness.

Reference Books......................

The Birder's Handbook: A Field Guide to the Natural History of North American Birds by Paul R. Ehrlich, David S. Dobkin, and Darryl Wheye. New York: Simon and Schuster, 1988.

California Insects by Jerry A. Powell and Charles L. Hogue. Berkeley: Uniersity of California Press, 1989.

California Mammals by E. W. Jameson, Jr., and Hans J. Peeters. Berkeley: University of California Press, 1988.

Discovering Sierra Mammals by Russell K. Grater. Yosemite Natural History Association and Sequoia Natural History Association in cooperation with the National Park Service, U.S. Department of Interior, 1987.

Lives of North American Birds by Kenn Kaufman. Boston, New York: Houghton Mifflin Company, 1996.

National Audubon Society Field Guide to California by Peter Alden and Fred Heath. New York: Alfred A. Knopf, 1998.

National Audubon Society Field Guide to Insects and Spiders, North America by Lorus J. Milne and Margery Milne. New York: Alfred A. Knopf, 1980.

National Audubon Society Field Guide to Reptiles and Amphibians, North America by John L. Behler and F. Wayne King. New York: Alfred A. Knopf, 1995.

National Geographic Field Guide to the Birds of North America, 4th ed., Washington, D.C.: National Geographic, 2002.

Parrots and Related Birds, 3rd ed., by Henry J. Bates and Robert I. Busenbark. Neptune, N.J.: T.F.H. Publications, 1978.

The Sibley Guide to Birds by David Allen Sibley. New York: Alfred A. Knopf, 2000.

The Sibley Guide to Bird Life and Behavior by David Allen Sibley, Chris Elphick, and John B. Dunning, Jr. New York: Alfred A. Knopf, 2001.

Smithsonian Handbooks, Birds of North America, Western Region by Fred J. Alsop III. New York: DK Publishing, 2003.

Stokes Beginner's Guide to Butterflies by Donald Stokes and Lillian Stokes. Boston: Little, Brown and Company, 2001.

Stokes Beginner's Guide to Dragonflies by Blair Nikula, Jackie Sones, Donald Stokes, and Lillian Stokes. Boston: Little, Brown and Company, 2002

Stokes Field Guide to Birds, Western Region by Donald Stokes and Lillian Stokes. Boston: Little, Brown and Company, 1996.

Index ....

About the Author and Illustrator.................

As curator from 1967 to 1979 at the Lindsay Wildlife Museum in Walnut Creek, California, **Gary Bogue** treated more than forty thousand injured and orphaned animals, pioneering the nation's first wildlife rescue and rehabilitation facility. His career in wildlife and environmental issues has also included stints as a community consultant, a founder of several professional organizations, and an executive director of a nonprofit pet welfare foundation, and he has been a regular columnist for the *New York Times* features syndicate and *Defender's,* the magazine published by Defenders of Wildlife. To date, Bogue has written a daily column on pets, wildlife, and environmental issues for the *Contra Costa Times* for thirty-two years. He lives in Benicia with his wife, two cats, a parrot, and a cockatoo, and he enjoys visits from his children, Jeff and Corey; his stepson, Karl; and his six grandchildren.

Chuck Todd is an award-winning illustrator whose work has appeared in newspapers, magazines, literary journals, annual reports, posters, and exhibits in California and the Midwest. He has been honored by the Society of Newspaper Design, Best of the West, the East Bay Press Club, and the California Newspaper Publishers Association. He is a full-time news artist for the *Contra Costa Times* and a freelance illustrator, and he also teaches drawing and storyboarding at the Academy of Art College in San Francisco. He lives in the Bay Area with his wife and two small daughters—his most ambitious projects to date.